MW00356183

Many Value *True Love That Lasts* And *The* Single *Question a Day*

Bishop of Bridgeport CT

Pope Francis is clear: marriage cannot be improvised. A good marriage takes commitment and hard work.**

In their book, Jim and Carol Steffen outline a very simple recipe for a strong, healthy marriage. By asking *one question a day*, husbands and wives can work together to build a relationship that endures. I invite couples of all ages and experience to take up Jim and Carol's challenge of growing true love that lasts using *the one question a day.*

—Most Reverend Frank J. Caggiano

*** When Bishop Caggiano received a special invitation from Pope Francis to work on the Synod dedicated to "Young People, Faith and Vocational Discernment," the Bishop thought so much of the book, he took a copy for the Pope.*

Best Selling Author

In a simple powerful way, this book will show you how to value and enjoy the relationship with your spouse more daily by asking just *one simple question a day....*

In the end, you will be excited about waking up in the morning, so you can serve your spouse rather than desiring to be served. *Wow! That says a lot about this book.*

—From the Foreword by ***Ken Blanchard***
co-author of The One Minute Manager

Very Frustrated Unhappy Wife

Two years ago my husband cheated on me. I was crushed and unforgiving. Regular counseling sessions were a time to complain about my husband. I read your book to prove you wrong! A simple question can't change what paid counselors couldn't.

However, as I read story after story in this book, I could not only see myself – even ourselves. I liked how the questions changed the involved couples. My husband agreed to read the book and start the questions.

I truly love the book sooo much!!! I have hope. I am smiling again.

—Alicia and Bob

(Last name withheld to protect the happy)

Busy Executive

Asking the *single question* is a loving, caring way to start our day. But the surprising thing for my wife and I is it focuses our thoughts in a loving, caring way for the entire day.

—Mark and MaryEllen Stealgraeve

University Professor

As a wife of more that 50 years, mother of three and college professor for 47 years, I strongly recommend *The Secret Growing of True Love That lasts* to you not only if you are young or married for years but even if you will pursue a single path in life. It will guide you to a loving improvement any relationship important to you.

This book will help deepen your self–knowledge, expand your awareness of others and build your own happiness.

—Prof. Margaret J. Sullivan

Student

Although students usually don't have a spouse, we are still surrounded with many meaningful relationships. This book gives a simple and easy (*just a single daily question*) guide that can grow and strengthen our relationships now and for the rest of our lives.

This is a very beneficial way of thinking, making us and the important people in our lives feel more appreciated, valued, inspired,` cared for and happier. It's a great way to live.

—Meryl McKenna

Organization Effectiveness Consultant

I finished your book and LOVED IT!!!! Highly enjoyable read! I thought of friends I would like to buy the book for.

I look forward to implementing the *question everyday.* After reading it I started that day. So positive and beautiful!!! Thanks for writing it. I hope it will change the tide of 50% divorce.

—Eileen Hahn
Organization Effectiveness Consultant

Very Busy New Mother

With a husband that works in a different state and four little children, I have many interruptions. However, once I started reading *True Love That Lasts* it was hard to put it down because it's so captivating that I just wanted to get to the end! I am looking forward to improving my marriage.

—Teresa Lazzara
Pre–schoolteacher

Team – Preparing Couples for Marriage

Asking *just one question* a day may seem too simple, but we promise that doing so will help build a foundation that is rooted in He (God) who make all things new.

Having watched hundreds of friends and family get married and stay married with varying degrees of success, we pray this book will find its way into the hands of all those preparing for this great sacrament of service.

—Patrick Donovan,
Executive Director, Leadership Institute
—Maureen Donovan,
Director of Events, NFCYM, Inc.

Executive Search Director

Quick Read! It made me take inventory of my marriage of 43 years. My appreciation of my wife's worth has faded over time. *A single question a day* seems a simple and easy way to change this, especially as Chapter 10 reads.

—Scott Williams

Worldwide Marriage Encounter

The WWME was tremendous. However, after a number of years I needed something more. The True Love That Lasts questions have been a godsend. I am enjoying my relationship with my spouse growing daily with the simplicity of the *single question a day.*

—Ed Dunn

Licensed Clinical Psychologist

The book is fantastic! What a delightful story of a seasoned husband and wife sharing their wisdom and insights with a young couple in love. This method reads as a synthesis of the "Love Languages", "Aligned Thinking" and the "Spiritual Exercises" of St. Ignatius Loyola – modern insights and time–tested spirituality.

At the right time this so *simple question a day* can be very helpful to psychologists in our work.

—Timothy G. Lock, Ph.D.

The Secret of Growing
True Love That Lasts

Forever and Ever
...And Then Some

The Secret of Growing True Love That Lasts

How a single question a day can help you love and enjoy your spouse more for a lifetime—starting immediately

(Or any other relationship important to you)

by Jim & Carol Steffen

Foreword by Ken Blanchard

Published Valentine's Day 2020

The Secret of Growing True Love That Lasts

How a single question a day can help you love and enjoy your spouse more for a lifetime—starting immediately

by Jim & Carol Steffen

Published by

ARKETT PUBLISHING
division of Arkettype
PO Box 36, Gaylordsville, CT 06755
806-350-4007 · Fax 860-355-3970
www.arkett.com

Published Valentine's Day 2020

ISBN 978-1-0878-6734-2

Printed in USA.

Cover photo by Nick Petrovic.

"Don't they (the media) realize that the family, all over the world, is in crisis? And the family is the basis of society! ***Don't they realize that young people don't want to get married?"***

Pope Francis, 2016 News Conference on Media

Dedicated to our Mothers
Spiritual and Physical
Who inspired and guided us

Our True Love Journey BTADCT

Before we met, we both dreamed of enjoying
True Love.
I invited you and you accepted.
Over time we became a couple.
After a time, you honored me, saying:
I was your *Better Than A Dream Come True.*
Slow to learn, when I finally realized I felt about you
the same way, I gave you a hat that said:
My BTADCT.
I also realized you always sign your special cards:

"Love, Forever and Ever and Then Some."

Still slow to learn,
I finally realized how blessed I am.
My dream of true love has
come true in and with you.
I also want Our True Love Journey to last

Forever and Ever and Then Some

From the authors' wedding invitation

CONTENTS

Appendix

Foreword

There are few if any relationships that are more important than marriage. Yet most people enter their marriage with little or no training on how to create a positive and long-lasting relationship. Enter Jim and Carol Steffen and their new book, *The Secret of Growing True Love That Lasts.*

I have known Jim for well over 40 years, ever since my teaching days at the School of Education at the University of Massachusetts/Amherst. I have always admired his creative ability to take a concept many people have trouble with and explain it.

He not only explains it, he clarifies it – like the concept of True Love – in a way that is quick-to-learn and easy-to-use so you can enjoy it immediately in your daily life.

In an environment where divorce was almost an everyday happening, Jim's loving marriage to Carol was a breath of fresh air. With almost 35 years to prove it, they have built a true love that has lasted the test of time. As a result it is only appropriate that Carol be Jim's co-author.

Why am I so excited about this book? Because my personal mission statement states:

> "I am a loving teacher and example of simple truths that helps and motivates myself and others to awaken to the presence of God in our lives and in the process realize we are here to serve, not to be served."

You might ask "That's nice, but so what?" After reading *The Secret of Growing True Love That Lasts,*

The Secret of Growing...

I guarantee you will learn what loving teachers and examples of simple truths Jim and Carol are. In a simple powerful way, they will show you how to value and enjoy the relationship with your spouse more daily by asking just one simple question a day.

Towards the end of your journey with Jim and Carol in this wonderful book, you will discover how growing a relationship with God can enrich your marriage even more.

In the end, you will be excited about waking up in the morning, so you can serve your spouse rather than desiring to be served. *Wow! That says a lot about this book.*

Thanks, Jim and Carol, for caring and really helping people grow love that lasts in their marriage.

Ken Blanchard
Co-author of
THE ONE MINUTE MANAGER and
SERVANT LEADERSHIP IN ACTION

Forever and Ever
...And Then Some

The Symbol

The book's symbol, like the book and life itself, can be viewed from two vantage points—The Present and The Big Picture.

The Present

Viewing the symbol from the present vantage point, the **heart** stands for one of our most basic desires: to love and be loved.

"True Love" reminds us that when we love and are loved, we want it to be love that is ***true***.

Once we experience True Love and ponder it deeper, we want this True Love to be infinite, symbolized by the infinity sign "**∞**"; i.e. a figure with no ending. To be *really never ending* we need to go to the good news of the Big Picture.

The Big Picture

"Forever and Ever...And Then Some" reminds us of the very good news of *The Big Picture.* Looking at life from the vantage point of *The Big Picture* reminds us that we are created in the image and likeness of our God, Who is—as St. John says—Love Himself. After a time enjoying the love of those we are close to here in this limited life, we will go back to our God of Love, from whence we came. There we will enjoy the love of those we love now and most especially *our God Who is infinite Love* ***"Forever and Ever...And Then Some."***

An "Aha" Bonus

This symbol, like every other part of the book, was reviewed by our advisory team. The first member of the team said the infinity symbol "∞" looks like you are looking at love through glasses. Then this "Aha" bonus jumped out. The symbol can also remind you that when you look at *True Love* through *infinite glasses,* you are seeing as God—who is infinite Love—sees, a God who has a vested interest in your marital success. (cf. Ch. 15 & 16)

Forever and Ever
...And Then Some

Introduction

Our Partnership

Writing this book, I though a lot about you, the reader. As we begin our journey to *Grow True Love That Lasts* together, we have a very real partnership. Like all partnerships, there is a common goal and areas of responsibility for each of the partners. Our common goal here is for you to quickly enjoy all the benefits my co–author Carol and I have enjoyed by asking just a *single question a day.*

My area of responsibility is to present you with a QEP—Quick-to-learn, Easy-to-use, Proven-to-work—process that can immediately help you Grow Your True Love That Lasts with someone you really care about. I can explain my area of responsibility best in the following three sections. From each section, there is a powerful *Take–Home Value* for your immediate use.

1. **A great experience—much can be learned**
2. **A miserable mistake—to be avoided**
3. **An even greater experience—to be imitated**

1. A Great Experience—Much Can Be Learned

My research for *Growing True Love That Lasts* began when I was working on my degree in philosophy. I asked challenging questions that you might have asked:

1. "What is *True Love*?" This challenge increased when I added:

2. "What is a *process or power* that can help me grow True Love?

After I got my doctorate and started my own business, I was blessed by interviews for some 45 years with thousands of very insightful people and recently been blessed with a wonderful team of advisors. (cf. list at end of book)

Those interviews added more questions to the challenge:

3. What process will not only increase True Love, but *grow it daily*?

4. Can this process *apply to anyone* you really care about: i.e. not only your spouse of one month or 50 years, but also present boyfriend, girlfriend, children, parents, friends, and even boss/worker/coworker?

5. Can this process help you avoid what happens to almost 50% of marriages, i.e. they end in divorce?

I'm happy to say the five questions/challenges above directly led to the discovery of the process that can *Grow True Love That Lasts.* This demonstrates the power of the questions you ask.

First Take-Home Value:
Asking the right question can produce great success.

2. A Miserable Mistake—To Be Avoided

My first marriage did not go well. Why? Seven or eight years into what began as a very happy marriage, I began asking, "Am I getting all I want/need from this relationship?" I did not have the Fact/Feeling/Request process you'll learn in Chapter 14 for asking my spouse for what I felt I wanted/needed in the relationship. This marriage ended in its ninth year.

I now understand I was asking the wrong question to improve the marriage and get what I truly wanted/needed. Much of the divorce was on my shoulders because I consistently asked the wrong question.

Second Take-Home Value:
Beware of asking the wrong question.

3. An Even Greater Experience—To Be Imitated

To receive the full value of this section *"An Even Greater Experience—To Be Imitated"* I first need to be very honest with you. And then you need to be very honest with yourself. There is good news, then bad news, then good news.

The Good News

Blessed with training in Philosophy and Theology and a doctorate in Educational Psychology and more that 40 years working with leaders in 160 Fortune 500 Companies, I was able to solve for the first time:

Five Life-Challenging Problems:

1. What is a *working definition* of True Love that we can build on?
2. Is it possible to *intentionally grow* True Love, even daily?
3. Is it possible to intentionally grow True Love not only daily, but with a *single question a day?*
4. Is it possible to ask your spouse for what you really want so that you not only avoid conflict, but actually *grow your relationship*?
5. Is it possible to accept *God's offer as Partner* to optimize your marital success?

As we tested the *single question a day,* I was delighted that the process was QEP—Quick-to-learn, Easy-to-use, and Proven-to-work—not only with each other, but with anyone dear to us—friend, parent, child, even worker/boss.

The Bad News

Even though my spouse and co-author, Carol, discussed with me and corrected everything I researched and wrote, she did not want to ask the so simple single question a day. *Now what?*

Carol is the person who created the brilliant True Love Symbol. Years before that, she helped me see that *life is better than a dream come true.* She was the one who taught me *Forever and Ever—And Then Some* and has signed all her cards to me that way for over 33 years, emphasizing her desire for True Love That Lasts, even beyond this life.

But she emphasized, "*A single question a day* is just not me!"

The Good News

Here is where I am being very honest with you. I'm the only one asking *the single question of the day* each morning. The good news for co-author and wife Carol and me is, we both benefit—though I think as the one asking the *single question a day,* I benefit the most.

Now for you to be very honest with yourself. There is a possibility that the one you love/care about—spouse, friend, child, parent, employee/boss—might not be interested in asking the *single question of the day.*

Now the good news for you—looking at the bigger picture – *this is Great!* Why? Because for you and the one you care about to enjoy all the benefits of asking the *single question of the day,* the choice is totally in your court. It's totally your decision. You might even be in a situation that you don't want to tell the one you love/care about that you are asking the *single question a day.*

In the ideal world, you and the one you care about both ask the *single question of the day.* And even at times share answers. ***But you don't have to!***

Again, the Really Good News, the decision is *totally yours.*

The Secret of Growing...

So I can honestly say as we begin our journey together, you can grow your *True Love That Lasts* even when you are the only one asking the *single question of the day*. You can anticipate *"An Even Greater Experience"* than you presently enjoy.

Third Take–Home Value:

- *Asking the right question at the right time can Grow True Love That Lasts—even daily.*
- *Each daily step takes you a little closer to your life becoming better than a dream come true.*

Your Responsibility as Partner

Like the young lovers in our story, John and Maria, I would like you to enjoy all the benefits the True Love That Lasts questions have to offer. But I have gone as far as I can go. Partner, the ball is *now in your court*!

For you to enjoy all the benefits like John and Maria, I need you to test the True Love That Lasts questions for *at least a month and beyond.*

Asking the True Love That Lasts question of the day with your spouse will be terrific. However, as I just shared and as Joan Jackson in Chapter 10 will share, asking the right question at the right time can work even if you are the only one asking that daily question.

I hope you will ask the *single question of the day* so I can guide you to:

- Grow Your True Love That Lasts *a little each day.*
- Make each day an easy step closer to living a life that is ***better than a dream come true.***

Chapter 1

The Proposal

If you watch the man pacing back and forth in front of Starbucks, you would suspect he was anxiously waiting for someone. Looking inside his heart, you would see he was *excited* and *more than a little nervous.*

Excited because he was going to propose to the drop–dead gorgeous fellow student, Maria, exactly 18 months to the minute when they first met.

He'll never forget that moment, 10:13 p.m. He had his latte and was leaving when Maria caught his eye. He was very bashful by nature, but her warm smile had invited him to join her as they both drank their lattes.

In the last 18 months, he learned that Maria was

- brilliant—soon to graduate summa cum laude with a degree in business psychology;
- an outstanding athlete—varsity softball pitcher;
- and a big hearted, very skillful organizer. The 'Give Back' organization she founded to support schools in Kenya would continue even after her graduation.

For John, Maria was a celebration of brains, beauty and loving, practical know-how.

She brought out the best in him. Considering himself very average—she made him feel very special like no one had ever done.

After dating for a year, Maria told him, "You're the most generous, giving person I have ever met. I really enjoy being with you, John, more than anyone. This has been the happiest year of my life."

For the last six months they had discussed being life partners and the family they would have after they got married.

John got the feeling Maria was waiting for him to "pop the question." He knew she loved surprises. Proposing at exactly 18 months to the minute from when they met would certainly be a great surprise for her.

At the same time, John was *more than a little nervous.* He had two huge concerns.

First, Maria was very concerned with all the people they knew who seemed to be happily married for a few years, only to *end in divorce.*

As a business psychology major, she knew that about half of those who married today would end up divorced on some tomorrow.

When John suggested living together for a time to get to know each other better, Maria immediately shared another statistic. Those who live together first before marriage have an even worse divorce record than those who don't. *Her fear of divorce* was his concern number one.

Concern two was her *not being there* the week before the big proposal. Because of her leadership, she was selected to represent their university at the conference:

How Graduates Can Live a Fuller Life in Today's Challenging World.

The day before she left for this conference, she had learned of Deming's *Kaizen*—continuous improvement—in her Business Psychology class. She asked John to explore this Deming's *Kaizen* while she was away because she saw it having great potential for them continuously growing their love and avoiding the divorce she so feared.

Maria explained, "At the end of the Second World War, products from Japan were seen as junk by most of the world. Edward Deming—an American—taught the Japanese *Kaizen*, 'the Continuous Improvement Method.' Adding a little improvement each day, today Japanese cars are seen as world quality. Would you check this while I'm gone?"

Maria continued, "If using *Kaizen*, the Japanese can change the world's view of their products from junk to top quality in just 55 years, we ought to be able to find a way to continuously improve our love relationship a little each day, so we can enjoy 55+ happily married years together.

"When we improve our love a little each day, we'd have a lifelong path to living a very happy, committed life together. And when we discover this path, we can help many others live a fuller—divorce free—life."

John thought, "This is typical of Maria, always also thinking of others." Excited about Maria's talking of spending *55+ happily married years together*, he spent hours checking out Deming and *Kaizen*.

Sure enough, as usual, Maria was right. Proof was so many Japanese cars on the road. John hoped they could find this lifelong path as an engaged couple.

As the week went on, *his anxiety* about her being absent before the big proposal concerned him more and more. In phone conversations she shared her excitement about what these world-famous speakers were presenting. He loved the practical action person she was. He feared what she might bring home from the convention that might mess up his 10:13 p.m. proposal plan.

When Maria arrived at 10:00 p.m.—all sweaty after jogging several miles, John was even more convinced she was drop-dead gorgeous.

As planned, at exactly 10:13 p.m. he got down on one knee and with the ring clearly evident said, "Maria, exactly 18 months ago to this minute, I met this wonderful drop–dead gorgeous person I would like to be my partner for life. Will you accept this ring?"

Maria's face lit up with a huge smile. John was thrilled and could not wait to hear "Absolutely!" or at least "Yes!"

Then the smile disappeared, and Maria said, "John, get up. Not now! Let me explain!"

CHAPTER 2

The Commitment

Maria clarified, "I do love you, but now is not the time.

"Let me tell you the exciting things I learned at the conference from world famous experts: Insights that can help us discover the lifelong path we want to grow our love daily and avoid the divorce trap."

John's worst fears were realized. "Now is not the time!" But he did find two very strong positives.

First, she did not say "No!" But "I do love you," followed by a hug and a kiss. Both helped raise his spirits.

Secondly, the 18 months' dating Maria had convinced him that, if she said the insights of these experts could help them discover the lifelong path she needed to say 'yes,' it was certainly true.

Maria continued, "Of the many great presenters, this world expert on happiness and living beyond 100, Dan Buettner, gave me insights that can change our life together. He said marriage happiness builds till about the first anniversary and then slowly begins to slip. He also said if you have a good reason to get up tomorrow, you can add years to your longevity.

"We need to find a lifelong path to grow our love—a little each day—for life. That would take advantage of his insights. It will certainly give us a good reason to get up tomorrow, which could add to our longevity—maybe be married 55+ years.

"And by increasing our love a little each day, we will not be one of his statistics of 'happiness beginning to slip' around our one-year anniversary."

John replied, *"55+ years with you* would be more than a dream come true; but wouldn't it be easier to find this lifelong path as an engaged couple? How do you propose to start to find this lifelong path?"

Focusing only on the lifelong path, Maria said, "I think Deming's *Kaizen* and continuous improvement offer us an excellent place to start. Did you check him out?"

"I did," John was delighted to say. "And, as usual, you are right. His Kaizen—continuous improvement—did guide the Japanese to move the world opinion of their products from junk to top quality in 55 years."

"I was sure I could depend on you," Maria replied with satisfaction.

"So why can't we use Kaizen to find the lifelong path to grow our love a little each day for the next 55+ years?"

John, now *absolutely delighted* she was talking of growing their love for the next 55+ years, found it easy to say, "We could. What else did you learn?"

Maria, excited with John's support, said, "We had a wonderful presentation on creating new habits. The presenter called it her *QEP Habit Builder.* To successfully create a new habit, the habit needs to be ***QEP***:

Quick to learn
Easy to use
Proven to work

"A Quick to learn,
Easy to use,
Proven to work
lifelong path to
help us
grow our love and
relationship
a little each day.

"On the plane flying home I thought a lot about our getting married. So, I put Deming, Buettner, and the *QEP* method to work to describe the lifelong path I would like us to discover and enjoy.

"John, will you join me in the excitement of discovering this lifelong path? Then we can implement it together."

John's emotions went from excited to overwhelmed and back to excited. "I'm excited to work with you for 55+ years, but isn't that goal a pretty high bar?"

That was the start of a long and loving discussion to find this *QEP* method:

as an engaged couple

or as a condition for becoming engaged.

After Starbucks closed, they continued to talk in Maria's dorm.

At 4:00 am, Maria proposed a compromise. "The most promising plan we have discussed is to find a couple that has been married very successfully for many years and find out their Secret.

"If for a month you will work with me to find that couple, at the end I'll consider saying 'yes'."

As John drove home, he pondered the last six hours. He wanted to drive home with a commitment to be married. It didn't happen. A downer!

He began to smile as he considered the bigger picture. He *had a commitment* with his most amazing gorgeous Maria to discover a path to grow their love a little each day for 55+ years. *A firm commitment.*

If Deming and *Kaizen* could help the Japanese change the world view of their products in 55 years, he and Maria should be able to grow their love a little each day for 55+ years.

But, is it even possible? Another downer!

Again, his thoughts of growing their love for 55+ years broadened his smile to as big as it could be. He became euphoric.

The driver stopped at the light next to him at 4:15 that morning and, even with the windows closed, heard: "55+ years with Maria, *a huge WOW!*"

Seconds later the driver could not hear John whisper, "Grow love—even a little—every day?"

Then John's euphoria crashed as he muttered, "*Every day* is impossible! *How can we do that*?"

Chapter 3

The Search for the Secret

Excited, John wanted to get started in the search for the Secret immediately. What better place to start than at work? John asked his boss if he knew anyone who had been married for a number of years, who was as much in love today as when they got married.

His boss looked at him for a minute with a funny smile. He finally said, "I know a lot of people who wish they could get divorced, but no one who seems as happy now as the day they got married."

At week's end when John and Maria reviewed the progress of week one of the Search for the Secret, it was 14 inquiries and zero results.

During the second week, Maria was sent to a lady who a number of people said was presently very happily married. Her reply surprised Maria, "I think my husband and I are happier now than when we got married—then it was mostly emotion and looks—now we love more, knowing the real persons we are.

"Today we have true love. But to get here was very painful and problematic. *I wouldn't wish that on anyone.*"

By the end of the second week the score was: 30 inquiries, 29 "I know no one," and one "*I wouldn't wish that on anyone.*"

At the end of the third week, while jogging together, they met Mr. Frickenschmidt, a friend of John's family. "Mr. Frickenschmidt," John said, "you seem to be happily married. What's your secret?"

Mr. Frickenschmidt immediately replied, "I don't have any secret."

Then he thought for a moment. "Come to think of it, I do have a rule of thumb. I just let the boss be boss and do what she says. That seems to keep peace. Why don't you go ask the boss? She's in the house making supper."

When Maria asked Mrs. Frickenschmidt the same question, the answer differed a little. "Secret? I don't have a secret. I do have a rule of thumb. I just let my husband think he is right all the time—even when it's obvious he's wrong. That keeps the peace and we are happy together."

As they got back to jogging, they laughed, agreeing that was not the secret they were looking for.

Maria added, "You know, I do think Mr. Frickenschmidt is a wise man."

John replied with a grin, "I rather thought Mrs. Frickenschmidt had a bit of wisdom."

At the end of the fourth week, after 28 days, the tally was 52 inquires:

__4__ replies to laugh about, __0__ secrets to live by.

Both John and Maria were disappointed. They agreed their search taught them three things:

1. There were not many couples who felt more in love now after many years than they did when they got married;

2. The few that did, either did not know how they got there or;

3. Didn't feel comfortable in sharing their secret.

They agreed to get together on day 31 and discuss options. John didn't like this "discuss options." He wanted to be engaged and not just in the search.

On day 30 Maria asked John to meet her immediately. She might have found what they were looking for in the local paper with a picture of a cake. John got there immediately wondering how a picture of a cake could help. The cake read:

"Still The Young Couple After 55 years"

Part of the article with it read:

Still The Young Couple After 55 Years

The friends and children of Carrie and Bill Kimmel insisted this couple—even though married 55 years—deserves the title:

"Still The Young Couple"

because they seem more in love than newlyweds. Carrie and Bill say it is all due to *The Secret of Growing True Love That Lasts.* They feel it's given them a Crystal Marriage.

They say the Secret is built on their definition of True Love.

And they say the Secret is so quick to learn and easy to use, people would not believe them if they shared it; even though it has surely created outstanding success for them for 55+ years.

Because they fear people will misunderstand the simplicity of *The Secret of Growing True Love That Lasts,* they refuse to say more.

They did say if a couple has the right attitude and is willing to try the Secret for 30 days, they would act as their coaches.

After reading the entire article, John said with excitement, "Maria, this couple is in the next town, just 20 minutes away. I'll call them and ask if they are willing to see us and how soon.

"I wonder if they will share their Secret with us.

"More importantly, what do we have to do to show them we have the right attitude and are willing to try it for 30 days or more?"

Chapter 4

How The Secret of Growing True Love That Lasts Helped Them Be "Still The Young Couple" Married 55 Years

When Maria and John arrived at Bill and Carrie's home, they were impressed; it was small, simple, and very neat. Certainly, a huge checking account was not *The Secret of Growing True Love That Lasts.*

After John and Maria were comfortably seated around the warm fireplace, Maria began.

"We understand from the newspaper article that all your children and friends said you deserve the title "*Still The Young Couple*" because you seem even more in love now than a newly married couple. We'd certainly like you to coach us to the same success."

Bill replied, "As the article also said, we would be glad to share the *Secret of Growing True Love That Lasts* to a couple with the right attitude and who are willing to try the method for 30 days. Tell us about yourself and what you're looking for."

John quickly explained the meeting, the proposal, the reason for the rejection and the commitment to find a model.

Maria then explained:

- her fear of divorce,

- her desire that they have True Love that will last,

- Deming/*Kaizen* and continuous improvement,

- how marital happiness can peak at one year

- the desire for a Quick, Easy, and Proven method of creating a habit that will grow true love a little each day.

Then Maria shared their goal, "Our goal is to find a *quick to learn, easy to use, proven to work lifelong path to grow our true love and relationship a little each day.* When we do, we hope to be, 'Still the Young Couple' when we are married 55 years, like you."

John—delighted to hear Maria mention *married 55 years*—added, "We would like to know what is *The Secret of Growing True Love That Lasts* and why do you feel you have a *Crystal Marriage?* What does that mean?"

Then Maria added, "And we would also like to understand *your definition of True Love.* I fear the emotions of the moment cloud True Love."

Carrie now talked for the first time. "Taking into consideration all you just shared, you certainly have the attitude that will make the *Secret of Growing True Love That Lasts process* work for you. If you are willing to use the True Love That Lasts process for 30 days, I'm convinced you will begin to enjoy a Crystal Marriage.

"Bill, I think we are ready to start."

Maria answered, "John and I are more than willing to give it a 30-day try. How soon can we begin?"

Bill replied, "Immediately. Your three very insightful questions are like stepping stones to better understand how the Secret works.

"We'll not only share the Secret; we'll have people who use it daily share their experiences and the benefits they enjoy. Let me repeat your four questions:

1. ***What is a Crystal Marriage?***

2. ***Why and how does the True Love That Lasts process lead to a very happy Crystal Marriage?***

3. ***What is a definition of True Love that works for us and can work for you?***

4. ***What is a quick to learn, easy to use process to grow True Love daily for a lifetime?***

CHAPTER 5

Why A "Crystal" Marriage?

Bill began, "To appreciate 'Why A Crystal Marriage' you need to understand Carrie's and my story.

"We met in our sophomore year in college and quickly became a couple. Carrie was a psychology major and I was in theology.

"At the beginning of our junior year, Carrie suggested we do a *Semester at Sea* the last semester of our junior year; leaving Vancouver, BC in February, arriving back in Florida in May, and getting a semester credit.

"Our parents weren't equally excited, but eventually recognized the benefits of world exposure.

"When we left in February, we'd known each other for 18 months. John, I understand your desire to be engaged. I wanted to return to Florida engaged. Carrie, share your situation, Tokyo, and my first proposal."

Carrie continued. "My parents divorced when I was in late grade school. When that happened, everything changed for me.

"I loved Bill and wanted to get married. Like you, Maria, I felt we had something very special and I wanted to build on that *specialness*. I needed time to clarify what being married-for-life meant. I feared divorce. I wasn't ready in Tokyo for a proposal."

Bill continued, "When I proposed again in Singapore in mid–March, Carrie said she wanted our specialness to be *transparent*—and said, 'Not now.'

"In mid-April I proposed again in Sydney. She pointed out that her parents didn't always level with one another—she wanted our specialness to *ring true* by always being very honest with each other.

"When I pointed out that I had always been very honest with her, she said..."

Then Bill turned to Carrie. With a smile, Carrie completed the sentence, "...I said, 'I know you have, but I'm still not ready." They all laughed.

Bill said, "We smile, even laugh today, but I was getting frustrated. I wanted to arrive in Florida engaged. After a fantastic time in Cape Town, South Africa, Carrie gave me the *Crystal Marriage Key* as we left.

"All alone, we sat on the back of the boat on a picture-perfect day—warm sun, a deep blue marshmallow cloud sky. As we watched the skyline of Cape Town disappear into the horizon, Carrie reviewed what I had shown her of Nelson Mandela's life and his wonderful forgiving spirit that built South Africa."

Carrie continued, "I said, 'The last couple days you brought out the best in me, Bill. I want to imitate Mandela's loving forgiveness. That's what I want our marriage to be—to help each other *sparkle with our best.*'"

Bill replied, "Listening closely, I knew she wanted our marriage to be *special* by being *transparent* and *ring true.* In the gorgeous setting, alone on the back of the boat, she gave me part three of being special, bringing out the best in each other, i.e. helping *each other sparkle.* I spent the time from there to the Rock of Gibraltar working out my plan. I decided the second day on Gibraltar would be the most romantic day. By then, we had seen all of the sights.

"I invited Carrie to a picnic at sunset on the southwest side of the Rock. With the Rock reaching to the sky behind us and the endless ocean in front of us, it was the perfect romantic setting for me to give it my all."

Carrie—with a broad smile—simply added, "The sun was setting as if for just the two of us!"

Bill continued, "There was nothing between us and Florida but water. My concern was, we would be in Florida in a few days. This was my last chance for the proposal. I pulled out all the stops.

"I said, 'Carrie, I know you want to get married as much as I do, but I also know you want to be sure because you want to avoid the mistakes of your parents who ended up in divorce.

"'I've come to see that you want a Crystal Marriage.' When I said, 'Crystal Marriage,' she looked at me with a big question on her face.

"That look said it all."

Bill continued, "Here is how I know. In *Tokyo* you emphasized we had something *special* and you wanted to build on that. You know Crystal is special because when we went to your grandmother's, she made events special by taking out her Crystal.

"In *Singapore,* you wanted our marriage to be special by being very *transparent.* Crystal is famous for its transparency.

"In *Sydney* you wanted our marriage to be special by *ringing true to each other.* Crystal, when pinged, rings very true and longer than just ordinary glass.

"After Cape Town you wanted our marriage to bring out the best in each other. Crystal takes any light in the room and makes it *sparkle.*"

Carrie had to jump in, "By this time I was so pleased with Bill. He had really listened to me. How could I continue to say 'No?'"

Bill—now smiling broadly—continued, "Crystal is very special down to its very molecular structure. Take carbon for example. Carbon is coal when the molecular structure is random.

"But when you have an event—like huge pressure that forces the molecular structure to become organized—you have a crystal. That special event takes the same carbon, crystallizes it and you have a diamond.

"I said, 'Carrie, you are already more valuable than a diamond; if you will say 'yes' and become *my diamond,* I'll agree we'll spend our senior year looking for *that event or process* that will organize our lives to give us a Crystal Marriage for life.

"'So, diamond of my heart, will you accept this diamond and become *My special diamond*?'"

Carrie, with a smile on her face and a tear in her eye said, "I was overwhelmed. With great joy I whispered, 'Absolutely yes!' and sealed the deal with a big kiss and a long hug!"

Carrie paused a bit remembering the moment. With a tear she added, "I was also impressed—Bill, a theology major, knew a lot about physics and being romantic.

"In the final analysis, saying 'yes' is a lot about trust. I really trusted Bill would follow through and find that special process by the end of our senior year. But in finding that special event, that special process did not happen automatically, as we will show you.

"Let me refresh your drinks. I think Bill wants to show you the exact sheet he used on that most memorable day. We both consider that sheet to be very special."

To Grow a Crystal Marriage With the Diamond of my Life

Crystal is:	**You want our marriage to be:**
Special in 3 ways:	Tokyo—special
1. Transparent	Singapore—transparent
2. Rings true	Sydney— speech rings true
3. Sparkles all other light	Cape Town—sparkle each other—bring out the best in each other
An event is needed to make it happen. Huge pressure organizes the molecules of carbon to make them a crystal—a diamond.	If you'll say "yes" we'll spend our senior year finding that *event* or process that will organize our daily lives to assure us of a Crystal Marriage for the rest of our life.

Chapter 6

What Is True Love?

Carrie continued their story. "We began the first semester of our senior year with great expectations. We were in search of the process that would give us the Crystal Marriage I wanted. We were enthusiastic because we had resources: Bill had his entire Theology department to ask for help and I had my Psychology department that could help.

"And we saw a double rainbow at the end of the year. First, we would be married and secondly, we could begin living the Crystal Marriage we were confident we would discover.

"Maria, your goal is to build your marriage on True Love. If Bill and I were going to grow our True Love daily, our definition of love needed to have three characteristics:

1. Operational—we needed to use it daily.
2. Simple—so we could remember and use it daily.
3. Gibraltar Rock solid—based on the research of the ages.

"To get all three, no small order! To do it quickly by the end of the semester—a real challenge."

Carrie continued, "Both Bill and I had to write final term papers. Luckily, our faculties agreed that we could write one paper. The benefit was our definition would work looking at True Love from both the Theology department—two thousand plus years of history—and Psychology department—the most modern insights of today. We found it easy to agree on the conditions, however, we did not see the problems keeping both departments happy would cause.

"Our title was: *A Practical View of True Love to Grow a Crystal Marriage.*"

Bill picked up the story. "We very quickly ran into the colossal problem I'm sure you can appreciate. Love is used in so many ways. Here are six; just a little sample:

- You love your new car—an inanimate object
- You love your dog or cat—a living being
- You love your friend—a person
- You love your spouse—a very special person
- You love God—a Divine person
- God is love—the essence of the divinity.

"This huge span made it both challenging and confusing! At times, there were theological, psychological, and practical disagreements between our departments that could have failed us.

"In the beginning it was easy to agree that our final definition would meet both the Theology and Psychology departments' standards. However, that agreement caused a huge problem and a battle between them.

"But in the end, the benefits exceeded the battle. Our final definition of True Love had a much wider use."

Bill continued, "Professor Reed from my Theology department was especially helpful in bringing the two departments together. When we ran into other relationship problems in our search for the process of building our Crystal Marriage, Professor Reed was critical—but more about those challenges to come later. He guided our review of the literature that went from before Aristotle to Pope Benedict's *God is Love* encyclical and included many nations. That meant that our review of literature covered more than two thousand years and at least five different cultures.

"When it was all over, both departments said they learned a lot. Here is what has served us well for these 55+ years."

Bill explained, "First, what love is not! It is not just an emotion. It can start with our emotions. It can include a lot of emotion and passion. Since emotions can't be turned on and off at will, if love is just an emotion, we could never grow our love daily, which was our dream.

Love begins when you first know the value of or appreciate someone or something.

"Many people use the phrase, 'I love my car—or cat—or job.' And it is meaningful. But for the purpose of growing True Love in our Crystal Marriage, we just focused on first knowing, then valuing or appreciating a person.

"You can value and appreciate a person for a multitude of reasons: they're good looking, smart, funny, they care about you, and on and on." He looked at Carrie, and smiled, "As my sweetie is!"

All laughed.

Bill continued, "For love to last, this value has to grow over time. A huge mistake many make that leads to divorce is forgetting that you need to work at growing the value of the beloved regularly. When that *value isn't growing, love is dying.*

"Dying love leads to unhappiness and eventually divorce. Our goal was to grow our True Love daily. When that happens, divorce becomes a non–question.

"Then love grows two ways. Once you value or appreciate the other, the first of the two ways is the *love of benevolence*, i.e. *you wish for and do good for the one you love.*

"A critical part of this love of benevolence is its double effect. First, the one loved receives the good wished for and/or done by the lover. In addition, the lover—because of the love and the union created by the love—receives the satisfaction of seeing the loved one pleased.

"Here's an example: surprising Carrie with a rose pleases her, the one loved. I'm delighted she is pleased and surprised because I love her.

"It's a trifecta win, a triple win from a single rose: Carrie wins, I win, and our relationship wins.

"The amazing aspect of true love is the lover takes the one loved into his/her value system, even into his/her heart. The one loved exists *in the lover in some real, exciting, wonderful way.*

"You can see it in many examples. The lover rejoices when the one loved rejoices and cries when the loved one cries. This leads to union, the third part of love, *the love of union.*

"Because you value and appreciate the one loved, you want to be with them. You consider it a privilege to be with them. This union can take many forms—physical, psychological, spiritual and sexual.

"The love of union is so important to complete the love of benevolence.

"A quick example. Suppose a person says they love their spouse and wants to do good for them, but doesn't want to be with them. Something very significant is missing.

"We were very happy that both the Theology and Psychology departments agreed on our practical operating definition of True Love."

Carrie summed up. "These are the three very simple, very useful parts of our definition of true love that the Secret of Growing True Love That Lasts is based on and the process that has let us enjoy a Crystal Marriage for these past 55+ years:

An Operational Definition of True Love

Love begins when you know, value, and appreciate the one you love.

Love of Benevolence

You wish for and do good for the one you love.

Love of Union

You want to be closer to and united with the one you love.

Bill added, "As we shared, writing the dissertation was a battle, even at times a battle between the Theology and Psychology departments. Emotionally drained, we really needed the semester break.

"However, we had a significant concern to deal with. We agreed by our wedding we would have a plan to create our Crystal Marriage.

- Special
- Transparent—to each other
- Rings true—truthful to each other
- Sparkles other light—makes our best shine
- Event to make it happen???

For carbon to go from coal to a crystal diamond, it needs the event of tremendous pressure.

We needed some event, some process that would quickly, easily and simply help grow our True Love daily. But what? How?

"Maria, we didn't say it the way you put it, but we were looking for exactly the things you are looking for, i.e. a lifelong path, quick-to-learn, easy-to-use, proven-to-work to value and enjoy our spouse, our relationship, more each day.

"The huge problem we were facing was our wedding was just five months away and we had *no idea of the next steps.*"

Maria, feeling their concerns, whispered "So, what did you do?"

CHAPTER 7

What is a Quick to Learn, Easy to Use Process To Grow True Love Daily for a Lifetime?

Carrie continued their story, "We were delighted with the simplicity of the operational definition of True Love we clarified in our dissertation, *A Practical View of Love to Grow a Crystal Marriage*. We took a deep breath.

"The January semester break was full of excitement as we began to prepare for our June wedding."

Bill jumped in, "In February panic set in. Our Gibraltar agreement was, by the end of our senior year—before our June wedding—we would have a plan in place to grow our love for the rest of our lives, so we could enjoy our Crystal Marriage; the lifelong path Maria wants.

"And we really like *your QEP* goal, that is quick to learn, easy to use, and proven to help grow love a little each day. It certainly has been proven to work for us all these years.

"At month's end, Carrie and I had no idea of the *event* that would help me deliver my promise. I didn't want to go into our June wedding not fulfilling my commitment to have a plan in place. Not a good way to start our desired Crystal Marriage.

"In March, I reviewed all I had learned in my theology work and Carrie did the same in her psychology area. We found nothing to help."

Carrie continued, "On April 1, Bill said he had a solution. Knowing Bill's desire to entertain me, I asked, 'Is this an April fools' joke?'"

Bill replied, "I told her no; I think we should go see Professor Reed. He helped us with the simplicity of our working definition of True Love and—most challenging—got the departments to agree. So, we set up an appointment.

"The Professor knew the story of our Semester–at–Sea and the WHY of the Crystal Marriage. He picked up on the *event*—the enormous pressure—that changes the carbon of coal into the crystal of the diamond. He said, 'You're looking for an event. Instead of enormous pressure, your event or process needs to be *so very simple* but still with huge power to direct your daily actions for life. Quite a challenge!'"

Bill continued, "The professor pointed out that many people like Ford, Edison, and the Wright Brothers had *quite a challenge,* but made great fortunes and created life–changing inventions for humanity by simply *asking the right question at the right time.* Ford was his favorite example.

"He said if we understood how Ford met his *quite a challenge* that gave him a huge competitive edge over other auto makers of his day, we would see the solution to *our quite a challenge.*

"In the early 1900's, Ford was like many of the 2,000 automakers around Detroit, asking himself how he could make an elegant car and get a corner on this huge market. He was looking for his significant competitive edge.

"At the time, his workers made about $1.25 a day and a car cost $800, or more than two years' salary. Totally beyond the reach of most of his employees!

"Then he changed his question to: 'How can I make an inexpensive car, so my workers can buy one?' Certainly quite a challenge.

"In answering his new question, Ford discovered the assembly line and put it into the production of his 1913 Model T.

"Eventually, because of the question he asked and the assembly line answer, the price of cars dropped from $800 to $350 and he was able to raise workers' pay to $5 a day. The cost of a car went from more than two years' salary to 14 weeks' pay.

"This question—Ford's *event*—gave him the significant competitive edge that made him very rich and millions got new model T's, all because of the power hidden in a single question.

"Could a single question a day be the *event* we needed? Could a single question a day give us the significant competitive edge to grow our True Love daily?"

John said with excitement, "So with the Professor's help, you created the True Love That Lasts—'*so very simple*' as you put it—questions. These are the questions I really want to hear."

Maria added with equal excitement, "If the event or process that gave you the Crystal Marriage is as simple as asking a few questions a day, it fits perfectly with our version of Deming's *Kaizen*.

"It could help us with our goal of improving our love a little each day.

"And it would fit our *QEP* desire. A few questions a day would be *quick* to learn and *easy* to use. And they will be *sure* to work as proven by your 55+ years of Crystal Marriage."

John, now very enthused, said, "Fantastic, how soon can we start? What are these questions? I'll write them down."

Carrie smiled to Bill who replied, "Your enthusiasm is great news for Carrie and me.

"I have a little bad news and a lot of good news for you.

"Maria, there are not a lot of questions for each day—only one. That is the bad news if you want to call it bad," he said with a grin.

He continued, "To make True Love That Lasts operational there are still a few challenges here, like:

1. What question should you ask each day?
2. Will they work if only one person asks the questions?
3. Do you have to tell the other person your answers?
4. Can you use them if you're not married or already married for years?

"Since we created the True Love That Lasts process to grow our love and enjoyment of each other, we are slightly prejudiced.

"The really good news is, we have a group of people who would be delighted to explain the question of the day to you and the benefits they immediately enjoy from it. If you could free up the next three evenings, we'll set that up for you."

Maria looked at John and immediately said, "We'd be so honored if you would."

Bill took care of it immediately. After he made a phone call, he made notes on a paper. Then he said, "The first couple, Pat and Harry, will be very glad to see you tomorrow evening. Here is your visitation schedule for the next three nights. After each visit, fill this out and then call us. We'll be anxious to hear how it went and give you directions for the next step." He gave John the schedule.

Maria and John's Visitation Schedule

Your Goal: *To discover a quick to learn, easy to use, proven to work path to grow your true love daily.*

Monday Appointment

Love begins *When you know, value, and appreciate the other person.* Visit with Pat and Harry

Monday and Thursday Question

Tuesday Appointment

Love of Benevolence: *You wish for and do good for the one you love.* Visit with

Tuesday and Friday Question

Wednesday Appointment

Love of Union: *You want to be closer to and united with the one you love.* Visit with

Wednesday and Saturday Question

Coaches: Carrie & Bill, honored to be called "***The Young Couple***"

CHAPTER 8

Can a Single True Love That Lasts Question Turn a Potential Divorce into a Crystal Marriage?

Early the next evening as they drove to meet Pat and Harry Dolesh, Maria reviewed the schedule and Bill's instruction. "Don't be put off by their surroundings. They've had life–changing problems. Does that mean money problems? Do they live in a shack?"

The first ten minutes of their visit, both Maria and John were continually amazed by:

- The 7,000 sq. ft. English Tutor crowning the hill
- The double carved mahogany front doors
- The free-standing spiral staircase highlighted by the brilliant crystal chandelier
- The double fireplace that you could walk through
- The racquet ball court in the triple garage
- The ballfield and toboggan chute for the kids

John was so wowed by the floor to 22' ceiling fireplace with glowing bronze stone that Maria whispered as she pulled him into the spacious family room, "Come, you're gawking!"

Comfortably seated with a drink, John said, "This is the third fireplace I've seen. Do you have one in every room?"

Pat, a friendly woman of mid–fifties, said with a smile, "If it were up to Harry, there would be. No, there are only seven, including a genuine bake oven in the lower level."

Just then Harry arrived all sweaty. "My little princess is too good for me. She got me three out of four in hand ball. Pat, have you shared much of our story?"

"No. I was hoping you would start."

Harry began, "Well, this home was Pat's dream. At the time we had two goals—raise the kids in a wonderful place and build her dream house. We did both.

"But there is more to life than your dream house on the top of a hill and all the pleasures money can buy. We got into a very bad habit." He pointed to a plaque left of the fireplace.

Teasing is not only okay,
it's great,
as long as the one teased
is still having fun.
A soon as that stops, teasing stops!

Harry continued, "You know the key is ask the right question at the right time. The huge mistake we made was to let our teasing get out of hand. We both eventually thought the right question was, 'How can I get one over on my spouse today?' We were unaware that winning the *I got ya* game violated our family rule. Worse, two competing in the game is a sure path to divorce. Pat, time for your favorite 'Aha.'"

Pat began, "Harry and I both had very good jobs. And as he said, our dream was this castle and giving our kids all they could want. We missed what has become my favorite 'Aha.'" She pointed to the plaque on the right side of the fireplace.

Love is a most wonderful living thing. Like all living things, it needs to be fed. If you starve love, it slowly dies.

Pat continued, "As Carrie and Bill's Professor Reed taught, the key is the question(s) we ask ourselves. We were starving our love and empowering our divorce by 'How can I win the *I got ya* game?'

"Like many before and after us, we did not realize this most dangerous game we were playing. All too soon we were totally aware of its results. About seven years ago, we were planning for a divorce and ready to tell the kids when fate intervened."

Harry continued the story, "My prostate was fifty-five years old and giving me great trouble. I refused to be serious about it. Finally, Pat—with the little love for me she had left—insisted that we go to the doctor together. The situation was worse than I'd thought. I needed an immediate operation.

"Telling the kids about the divorce would have to wait. Before the operation, the doctor warned it was very serious and I might not make it. His suggestion to update my will was chilling. It changed our value system."

Pat picked up the conversation, "We began to seriously consider maybe there is more to life than a dream house and getting everything else that we want. Maybe we need to consider more basic things in our plans, like building our love relationship with each other and the welfare of our children."

Harry added, "The problem wasn't the dream house, it was the dreams of the dreamers and their attitude about the journey of life."

Pat continued, "The doctor's warning was so right. The hour-long operation developed complications. It took three hours with two specialists called in. Harry ended up in the intensive care unit, with no visitors at first. After the doctor gave me the bad news, he said he hoped I could see Harry in four or five hours. Not knowing what to do or where to go, I just sat in the waiting room and cried."

Maria and John were feeling Pat's pain so much that they forgot themselves and their questions for the moment.

Pat interrupted the flow of the story by saying, "Let's stop for some refreshments. Then we'll tell you how that cry was one of the best, not only of my life, but of our entire family's lives."

Chapter 9

Question One:

The Beginning of True Love!

Can a Simple *Question Change a Life?*

When everyone was refreshed with a cold drink and a variety of homemade cookies, Pat started. "This lady came over, sat next to me, and in a very supportive voice asked, 'Can I help?'

"That was Carrie. Bill was in for a similar operation, without the complications. Over the next couple days, Carrie became my major support person. The kids were great, but Carrie could help in a way that was totally beyond what they could offer.

"On the third day, when Harry was out of the ICU, I told Carrie everything that we have just shared with you. She asked me what questions I was asking myself. I didn't even know I was asking myself questions.

"With her help, I discovered the question I was asking was 'How can I get one over on Harry today and win the *I got ya game*.' Without even knowing it, I was asking a key question that was guiding me to this path that leads straight to certain divorce.

"Harry had similar talks with Bill when they shared a room.

"We accepted their offer to coach us in applying the *Secret of Growing True Love That Lasts.* When we began to implement their suggestions, things began turning around immediately. Don't get me wrong. It wasn't easy, right Harry?"

Harry smiled, "It wasn't easy—because change is always challenging. If there was an easy part—besides the support of Bill and Carrie—it was the *so very simple* single question of the day. Implementing the answer gave us total freedom.

"We understand and use the entire Secret, all the questions. However, Carrie asked us to focus on the Monday/Thursday question—where it comes from, the importance of the right goal and several of the attitudes that make it work. Maria, Bill explained you are interested in a version of *Kaizen*—continuous improvement in love daily. I think you'll find all the questions fit perfectly.

"The first question comes from how True Love begins. Remember Carrie and Bill shared with you, '*Love begins when you know, value, and appreciate the other person*'? The fact that the Monday/Thursday question is built on that very simple start of the definition of True Love makes it *so very simple.* Here it is."

Forever and Ever
...And Then Some

The Monday/Thursday Question

How can I value and appreciate the one I love (my spouse) more today?

John, silent for the moment, left space for Maria to exclaim, "Wow, truly *so very simple* and so straight forward!"

Harry said, "*So very simple,* straight forward—absolutely—but within that simplicity is the *power to quickly be life changing.*

"Instead of focusing on 'Am I getting all from this marriage as I deserve?' this simple question began to change my appreciation and love for Pat even before I left the hospital. When I asked that question, I saw how Pat was at the hospital every day. I saw how she was really worried about me even though we had discussed divorce. When we got home, I saw how she planned a welcome home with both boys and my little princess."

Pat continued, "The next Monday morning, after the kids went back to school, Harry put his arm around me, and told me all that and more. You know, for the first time in many years, I remembered why I had wanted him to propose."

John asked, "What happens if you can't think of anything more to appreciate? After all, you have been doing this for seven years now. Doesn't it get tiresome?"

Harry answered, "John, let me answer in three ways. First, we need love to live and it is a living thing. Like Pat's plaque says, *'Love is a most wonderful living thing. Like all living things, it needs to be fed. If you starve love, it slowly dies.'* Answering the Crystal Marriage questions are a *so simple way* to feed love.

"Secondly, I have never found a day when I could not find something new or different to appreciate about Pat, if only—that she made supper for me every day last week. Here it is Monday and she did it again." They all smiled.

"The third thing is a benefit that surprises me. When Carrie and Bill were helping us understand the True Love That Lasts questions, I feared I would have to give up my selfish question, 'Am I getting all I need from this marriage?' But to be honest, when I find something more every Monday and Thursday to appreciate and value in Pat, I don't need that selfish question.

"There is a hidden win-win here that I never imagined. Pat benefits because I appreciate her more. But to my great surprise and delight, I benefit because I have more to love. And you'll be glad to know related to your *Kaizen* process—it does grow love a little each day!"

With a broad smile Pat added, "When Harry is reflecting on his answer to his Monday/Thursday question, I find it easy to ask and answer my Monday/Thursday question also. Whereas, in the past our contest of *I got ya* just sparked increased competition to discover more *I got ya's;* this competition to find more to love is also contagious. But unlike the *I got ya* game, delightfully contagious.

"There is a power yet simplicity in asking the right question at the right time. The True Love That Lasts process is built on both that simplicity and power. In no place does the Secret of Growing True Love That Lasts say you must answer the question in this way or that. Or you must do this or that. It is totally free.

"Your answer is totally up to your creativity. You own the answer. You own the implementation. Here is freedom!"

Harry added, "And if you're not getting what you want, that is what the fourth question is for. Bill and Carrie said they felt something was missing around their tenth anniversary. That's when they discovered the last question that relates to sharing and asking what you really want or need."

Pat immediately jumped in. "Harry, what did Bill ask you to focus on, and does that include question four?"

Harry, a bit embarrassed, smiling replied, "Oops! Please cross that last remark from the record. But there is a lesson here. In the past, Pat would have reacted like, '*I got ya!* You screwed up again!' Now you can see, it's okay to help each other get things right."

Pat added, "That's right. One of the things I wanted to point out about Harry is, he is the first to admit he is not perfect. And he really cares. Because he cares for our kids, they have a racquetball court in the garage, a full ballfield in back for warm weather, and a toboggan slide for the winter.

"Maria, when you came in, you noticed the beautiful crystal chandelier in the foyer. Harry bought that for me to remind us that we are a Crystal Marriage family."

Harry added, "John and Maria, there is one more aspect of the Secret of Growing True Love That Lasts that needs to be considered. Our kids. They were not blind. They could tell that Pat and I were not the best of friends as our *I got ya* competition escalated. When we installed the crystal chandelier and explained why to the kids, their only remark was, 'We can see and feel the difference after you started using the True Love That Lasts questions regularly. *We like what we see and feel.*'

"A very simple statement. Very little said! But when you think what their lives would have been had we not met Bill and Carrie, that '*we like what we see and feel'* is enormous. In a few words, it captures a shift in what our relationship as a family will be for the rest of our lives. The single question a day has actually changed not one, but five lives!"

Pat added, "There's another benefit here—not one you are interested in right now, but hopefully eventually. You can use the True Love That Lasts questions related to *any relationship that is important to you.* I used it related especially to my two sons. At times they were a pill, and a *so very simple* question a day really made the difference. Using the question with the boys has helped me appreciate them more and I'm convinced the relationship I enjoy so much with them is because of the True Love That Lasts questions. I'm sure they don't even know that I do it. And that's okay."

Harry added with a beam, "By using the questions related to my mother-in-law, I love her more today than in years past. I'm sure that makes Pat and my mother-in-law's life happier.

"One last thing. Bill pointed out to us the challenge of the person we get up in the morning—the person we want to be—the reflexive self—or the person that just gets up and goes—the get–going self. The get–going self rarely gives any consideration to the person they really want to be today.

"In the past I got up as the get–going self. Without being aware of it, I fell into the trap of getting up to play the *I got ya* game. The True Love That Lasts questions have given Pat and me a *so very simple, yet so very powerful* method to get up as the reflexive self and live life as the *person we want to be.*"

After a moment to consider the magnitude of his last statement, Harry asked, "Any more questions?"

John replied, "You certainly have given us a lot to consider. Maria?"

Maria added, "The *so very simple* first question fulfills our QEP criteria: Quick to learn, Easy to use, and Proven to work, like it has for you. I hope the rest of the questions are as QEP."

Harry concluded the visit. "We have found them to be; I'm sure you will also. If you have any questions in the future, we would be more than honored for you to call or come back."

When leaving, Maria thanked them with, "Bill said you would humbly answer all our questions. Your sharing has been so generous and complete, you've answered questions even before we thought of asking them. We thank you for that and will consider calling if we have any more."

Maria drove as John began filling in the schedule for Pat and Harry and completed his notes. At the end of the circular drive, he said, "Stop for just a moment. I just want one more look at this Tudor home Pat called Castle Hill. It is! Those three chimneys make you feel like you are in front of an English estate. The only thing more wonderful is the couple who built it and the way they grow their True Love today."

John finished his notes as Maria drove home. As soon as he finished, they immediately called Bill and Carrie. They could not wait to report on all that they had just experienced and to receive instruction for Tuesday's visit.

John's notes looked like this:

Maria and John's Visitation Schedule

Your Goal: *To discover a quick to learn, easy to use, proven to work path to grow your true love daily.*

Monday Appointment

Love begins *When you know, value, and appreciate the other person.* Visit with Pat and Harry
The 'I got ya game' was leading to divorce. The True Love That Lasts questions saved their marriage; their three children living with two parents.

Monday and Thursday Question
How can I appreciate and value the one I love more today?

Tuesday Appointment

Love of Benevolence: *You wish for and do good for the one you love.* Visit with

Tuesday and Friday Question

Wednesday Appointment

Love of Union: *You want to be closer to and united with the one you love.* Visit with

Wednesday and Saturday Question

Coaches: Carrie & Bill, honored to be called "***The Young Couple***"

Critical Insights to Remember

1. *Love, like any living thing, needs to be fed regularly to continue to grow. If you stop feeding it, it stops growing and starts to die.*

2. *The answer and how to implement the answer are totally up to the one asking the question. The True Love That Lasts questions offer great freedom.*

Quadruple Benefit

1. *The one asking the question finds and enjoys more to appreciate and value in the one loved.*

2. *The loved one is appreciated and valued more.*

3. *It is easier for the loved one to respond in kind.*

4. *The relationship grows.*

CHAPTER 10

Question Two:
The Love of Benevolence—
Can Just One *Person Make It Work?*

When John picked up Maria the next evening, the first question he asked was, "You've had a night to sleep on our visit to Harry and Pat; of the many things they shared, what jumps to mind?"

With no hesitation, Maria replied, "I've been thinking about this all day. My answer has three parts. First, the question, *How can I appreciate and value my love more today,* is so simple. Second, the one asking the question receives benefits almost immediately when asking the question. And the third part is the *loved one* also benefits even if they are not there or aware of the question.

"John, what most impresses you?"

"I agree with all you said. But what impressed me most was how a simple question a day changed two people's lives almost immediately and for the rest of their life."

Maria replied, "Agreed. But I would change that two to five. In fact, the three kids could well be benefiting long after their parents have graduated to heaven. They'll be less likely to get divorced."

Maria continued, "A couple insights to remember as we consider our future. But now we need to talk about tonight. Let me review Bill and Carrie's suggestions.

"They said the Jacksons will share with us the second question, built on the Love of Benevolence. Like with the Doleshes, the Jacksons encourage us to ask any question, no matter how personal."

When seated comfortably with refreshments, Joan began, "We heard Bill and Carrie talk about ten years ago at a convention sponsored by Dan's company."

Dan added, "Our company president is a very practical and savvy guy. In the introduction, he said he invited Bill and Carrie because the better the personal life, the easier it is to be 100% in the business life when it is business time."

Joan continued, "I invited Dan to be here because I'm the only one who actually asks the questions and I get more benefits than Dan does. I'll show you by crazy 3/3 vs. 2/3 math.

"On the way home from the convention on the plane, Dan and I had a transparent, ringing true talk, two of the reasons they said a Crystal Marriage was special. I was excited to join Carrie and Bill. Dan wasn't! I asked him to be here today, so he could share his feelings with you firsthand. Dan, could you share your point of view?"

Dan picked up their story. "In their presentations, three of the most important things for me were: The Crystal Marriage is built on True Love, freedom, and it can work if just one person asks and answers the questions.

"Being a salesperson with a quota, irregular hours, and a lot of travel, I just felt asking even one more question a day pushed my bandwidth to breaking. I'm convinced Joan and I have True Love, and I encourage her to ask and answer the questions. And she agrees to honor my freedom, which I deeply appreciate."

Maria asked with concern, "Joan, don't you feel this is one sided?"

Joan smiled broadly and answered, "I had three choices:

- With Dan
- Without Dan
- Don't do it at all.

"Of course, I would like him to ask the questions, and in a way, you will see he does. But it was more important for me to honor the freedom of the True Love That Lasts method and let Dan be Dan. You'll see from my crazy math that we both win, but I win the most. I'll give you an example in a minute.

"In Bill's talk, he emphasized the True Love That Lasts method is built on—as the name indicates—True Love. True Love gives you freedom. I admired that a lot. He said it would work if only one person asked and answered the questions. Our experience says he was right!"

Joan continued, "As you recall from your notes, the Love of Benevolence is *you wish for and do good for the one you love.* My Tuesday/Friday question—as Bill likes to call it, the *so very simple* question—is built on the Love of Benevolence:

The Tuesday/Friday Question

How can I please and surprise the one I love (my spouse) more today?

Joan continued, "Asking this question, I benefit in many ways. Here is one of the clearest ways where my crazy 3/3 vs 2/3 math works.

"Dan likes surprises—I hate them! So, for his fiftieth birthday, I surprised him with the birthday party of birthday parties. I had friends invite us to an old-fashioned square dance. When we got there, I had arranged the square dance just for him with five sets—not five people—but sets of people to surprise him: his relatives, friends, our neighbors, his business associates, and even some of his old college buddies."

Dan picked up, "I must admit I was not only totally surprised; I was in shock. She had recruited one leader for each group:

- For relatives, it was my brother.
- For our neighbors, it was the couple next door.
- For my friends, it was my best friend.
- For my old college buddies, my senior class roommate.
- For people at work it was my boss, of all people, who really enjoyed surprising me.

"It took me hours to realize all the groups who were there. And it was even a week later when we reviewed the video that I realized how she did it.

"Yes, she even had a volunteer video the entire surprise, including the look on my face when all five groups came from nowhere and sang, 'Happy birthday!'"

Joan turned to John. "I'm enjoying the surprise just retelling it and listening to Dan just now. Consider the score. This time, for months I enjoyed working with these five leaders as we prepared the surprise. Again, I was thrilled 3 for 3, before, during and after the surprise. Dan just 2 for 3, during and after."

Maria, still sympathetically concerned, asked, "It is obvious you really enjoyed that event. It doesn't seem to upset you that you are the only one asking the questions? And isn't there a way that you can get what you really want on occasion?"

Joan replied, "There certainly is! However, Bill asked me to clarify the benefits both Dan and I receive when *only I regularly ask* myself the first three questions, focusing especially on the Tuesday/Friday Love of Benevolence. There is a way to tell Dan what I really want, but that relates to question four, the Sunday question.

"As Bill and Carrie were preparing for their tenth anniversary, they began to feel that something—maybe a lot—was missing. They asked that I leave those problems and *question four* for them to share.

"Do you have any other questions?"

John, always quick to respond said, "Joan, I like your crazy math. I prefer to call it winning math. Maria, what do you think?"

Maria replied, "My business psychology studies make me all too aware that about half the people getting married today will be divorced on some tomorrow. As Bill or Carrie might have shared with you, our goal is to find: ***A quick to learn, easy to use, proven to work lifelong path to help us grow our love and relationship a little each day."***

To Maria's surprise Dan jumped in, "Bill explained your situation when he asked us to see you. Being in business I'm very aware of Deming's *Kaizen* influence on Japanese products and how the Americans use it now. You're in very good company using Deming's *Kaizen* for your search."

Joan added, "Carrie also explained your desire to build on True Love. We also know the Doleshes. Pat's plaque emphasizing that True Love is a living thing *that must be fed is* right on.

"I have discovered that Bill and Carrie were right. True Love starts by focusing on the Monday/Thursday question, *how can I appreciate and value the one I love (my spouse) more today.*

"We were married twenty years before we met Bill and Carrie. In the seven years since, I have come to appreciate and value Dan more today than in the first twenty years, due in part to the Monday/Thursday question."

Dan replied smiling, "I'm not sure how to take that. It took twenty years for my true value to surface—and even then, it took help from Bill and Carrie to appreciate me."

When the laughter died down, Joan continued. "Jokes aside, because I put the True Love That Lasts questions where I start my day and ask the question of the day regularly, I feel my True Love of Dan has grown. I have a more wonderful husband to love today than seven years ago. And I feel—even though he does not ask the questions formally—he does reply in his own way."

Dan said nothing, but nodded approval.

Joan concluded the visit, "If in your search you have more questions, feel free to call any time."

As Maria drove, John completed his notes.

When he finished, he turned to Maria and said, "There is a simplicity and a complexity here. The working definition of True Love and the first two questions are very simple—*so very simple*—as Bill likes to say. The complex part is the almost endless ways they influence and build relationships. We've seen the same things in the Doleshes and Joan and Dan Jackson."

As they drove, they called Bill and Carrie to share much of what they learned and receive the directions for the Wednesday meeting. Their excitement made the discussion into a driveway discussion—it lasted so long they stayed in the driveway for awhile to finish it.

Maria and John's Visitation Schedule

Your Goal: *To discover a quick to learn, easy to use, proven to work path to grow your true love daily.*

Monday Appointment

Love begins *When you know, value, and appreciate the other person.* Visit with Pat and Harry

The 'I got ya game' was leading to divorce. The True Love That Lasts questions saved their marriage; their three children living with two parents.

Monday and Thursday Question

How can I appreciate and value the one I love more today?

Tuesday Appointment

Love of Benevolence: *You wish for and do good for the one you love.* Visit with Joan and Dan

The questions work even when just Joan asked them. Dan benefits but Joan feels the benefits most. 3 of 3 vs. 2 for 3.

Tuesday and Friday Question

How can I please and surprise the one I love more today?

Wednesday Appointment

Love of Union: *You want to be closer to and united with the one you love.* Visit with

Wednesday and Saturday Question

Coaches: Carrie & Bill, honored to be called "***The Young Couple***"

Critical Insights to Remember

1. *The true Love That Lasts method emphasizes great freedom as to how the questions are answered.*

2. *There is also freedom for just one partner to ask and answer the questions.*

Benefits to be expected

1. *Both benefit when just one person asks the question.*

   The one asking benefits the most before, during, and after–3/3.

   The other just during and after–2/3.

2. *It is easier for the loved one to respond in kind even if they are not asking the questions.*

3. *Using Kaizen, the relationship grows daily.*

Chapter 11

Question Three: The Love of Union— How to Live Life to the Fullest NOW?

As John drove to meet Ray Chambers, Maria reviewed the instruction for the evening. "Bill and Carrie said this interview will be unique. It will be only with Ray Chambers as Eleanor has passed away. There are three things they suggested we focus on:

1. Eleanor and Ray were one of the happiest couples they had ever met. Eleanor especially taught Ray, and then Bill and Carrie something about living life to the fullest. They especially wanted us to hear this firsthand from Ray.

2. Despite many challenges, they were still very happy.

3. They also applied the Love of Union in a very successful way, taking it to new heights because of Eleanor's attitude of living life to the fullest. Bill and Carrie want us to hear it firsthand from Ray."

John added, "Remember, as usual, Bill said we can ask Ray any questions. He really wants to share his story with us."

Ray's home had a garage on the first level. As Maria and John walked up the steps to the second level porch, Ray met them.

Tall and thin in his late sixties, Ray's smile was very welcoming. He said, "On such a pleasant warm, low humidity evening, let's have our drinks here on the porch. In a half hour there will be a beautiful sunset over the fields."

With each of them comfortable in their own rocker, John and Maria reviewed the three things they should look for.

Ray, smiling replied, "I've admired Bill and Carrie ever since we met them over twenty years ago. Let's begin with 'the happiest couple' and what Eleanor taught me, and eventually them, about living life to the fullest.

"When Eleanor and I were dating, Saturday night was our date night and this little hill was our favorite picnic spot. When a developer started to build, I quickly bought this; and when funds were available, built this house.

"I was an uptight fellow. I so much-admired Eleanor—or Babe—as everyone called her. She seemed to be able to have fun and a wonderful time no matter what. She would say, 'Ray—relax a little. Enjoy the moment!'

"After that happened more than once, I said one night, 'Babe, I agree with you. I wish I could relax more and enjoy the moment like you! If you'll share your secret, I'll try it.'

"With that big Babe smile she replied, 'No secret! But I do work at it. Let me think on it and I'll share next Saturday.'

"The next Saturday, just about this time before the sun dropped below the fields, she said she gave my question a lot of thought. She handed me this well-worn card."

This Moment

It's a gift from mom, dad, and Daddy.

I've been freely given this moment. Use it!

Not sure how many more I'll be given.

Celebrate this one for Rosie.

"Babe explained. 'Since high school, I've begun my day having a cup of coffee, reviewing this card, and spending ten minutes to plan my day to live the contents of the card.

"'The first two are facts anyone can use. The third I wouldn't wish on anyone.

"'Fact one: *This Moment: It's a gift from mom, dad, and Daddy.*
There was a time when I was not. Then, totally as an unmerited gift from Daddy—my favorite name for God—with the help of my parents, I was conceived.

"'I even have a picture of Mom and Dad on their wedding day above my favorite chair to celebrate the event. I like to think their loving each other is *me*.' When she said that, she smiled, obviously delighted with the thought.

"'Fact two: I've *been freely given this moment. Use it! I'm not sure how many more I'll be given!*
I know I have this moment to use most any way I want. I don't know about tomorrow or the next moments. So, I want to live this moment to the fullest, having fun with those around me if possible.'

"'The part I wouldn't wish on anyone I'm reminded by *Celebrate this one for Rosie.*
Rosie was one of my kid sisters, one of the twins. She died at seven. At her funeral I promised her I would live every moment of my life to the fullest and have all the fun that she missed for her.

"'When you know someone so close and younger than you, it makes it easier to live fact two: I've *been freely given this moment. Use it! I'm not sure how many more I'll be given!*?'"

Ray continued, "We all know people younger than we are who ran out of time before us. Their journey has ended. From the time Babe shared this, I tried to imitate her. She helped me make great progress, but I was never as good as her.

"The amazing thing for me was, Babe took the tragedy of her little sister's dying early and made it into a huge motivator that eventually helped many, including Bill and Carrie.

"When Bill and Carrie noticed how she was able to live each moment and life to the fullest, they asked how she created and maintained that attitude. She shared her story. She also shared the key to her success was the card, placed where she started her day, making it easy to review every day. She said without the daily review, she would forget.

"Bill and Carrie were so impressed; they made their own card and adapted the practice."

John, who usually could not wait to hear the *so very simple* question of the day, for the moment totally forgot that. Intrigued, he asked, "Was she very religious?"

Ray replied, "Not especially. She was a fun-loving realist who was totally committed to keeping her promise to Rosie and living the two facts she felt everyone could imitate."

There was a pause to ponder as John started his notes.

Ray broke the silence with, "I think the next thing on your list is: *Despite many challenges, they were still very happy.* Like most couples, we did have our problems. The first was our second child, Barbara Rose only lived two minutes. Babe refined her daily card to:

This Moment

It's a gift from mom, dad, and Daddy.

I've been freely given this moment. Use it!

Not sure how many more I'll be given.

Celebrate this one for Rosie

and Barbara Rose.

"When I got pneumonia and was out of work for six months, even though challenging, she still celebrated each day with great faith. She would say, 'Daddy, who made us in the first place, will take care of us in the second place.' He did.

"As I reflect now, because she lived a daily, moment to moment practice of appreciation, she lived her life to the fullest, like her cup was running over with gifts. Because of her attitude, her cup *was* running over with gifts. She taught me a lot. I think that is what Bill and Carrie wanted me to share firsthand."

After a short pause, John said, "I think we're ready for question three. Bill said because of Eleanor and her attitude, you were able to take the Love of Union to new heights. Can you explain what he means?"

Ray replied, "I'm sure you remember the Love of Union is: *You want to be closer to and united with the one your love.*

"The Wednesday/Saturday question is built on that."

Forever and Ever
...And Then Some

The Wednesday/Saturday Question

How can I be closer to and united with the one I love more today?

"Babe and I found Bill and Carrie's working definition of True Love not only very inspiring, but motivational. We were convinced The Love of Union is the crown or natural pinnacle of all love.

"When we found more value to appreciate in the other as a result of the Monday/Thursday question, the most natural thing was to want to be closer to and more united with the one loved.

"When the Tuesday/Friday question encouraged us to please and surprise the one loved, the most natural thing was to want to be closer to and more united to the one loved.

"Babe and I felt being closer to and more united was truly the *crowning glory, the apex of True Love.*"

Ray continued to explain, "Here is where Babe's *Fact Two* so prepared us to take union to a higher level. Fact two is: you have this moment. You don't know how many more you will have. What assurance do you have that you will use future moments—if given—to their fullest?" Bill stopped briefly to let John and Maria ponder his question.

He then continued, "The best assurance that you will use to the fullest *all* the rest of the moments you will be given is to *use this one to the fullest.*

"Applying this fact two to *union,* we didn't know how many days, moments we would have together. Everyone knows that their moments will end. Sooner or later we all need to graduate to a better life. But today we can live this moment and the opportunity for union to the fullest now. And we did!

"We spent time with the kids. But we also made time for just us. When we learned The True Love That Lasts questions from Bill and Carrie, the kids were 11, 9, and 7. My mom and dad and an unmarried sister lived just two doors north. They were delighted to take the three grandchildren.

"Their help made it easy for just Babe and me to do things together. We learned to dance. We biked with and without the kids. I was so blessed to experience this realistic fun lover, who valued growing relationships from so many aspects of union.

"My company was open Saturday mornings. Being one of the lower seniority members, I got the Saturday morning shift. I had Wednesday afternoons off. With the kids in school, Babe and I began taking naps together. Those were great for many reasons including making love.

"About three years after we heard Bill and Carrie talk, we were expecting again. This was a very happy time. Babe's parents, who had many grandchildren were thrilled. My parents who had only our three grandchildren, were *really* thrilled.

"The most thrilled person was Babe. Many times she told me, 'Ray, we're bringing new life into existence that will last for all eternity.'

"All went very well. We had our fourth little girl—of course, we'd lost one—but things were just great with one boy, now 14, and three little girls—12, 10, and the baby. Everyone was thrilled, especially our son. He insisted on holding the baby for the baptism.

"Things continued to be great right up to the six-month checkup after the birth. Babe was feeling a bit tired with loss of appetite. The doctor did tests. When he presented the results, he was very serious. 'Mrs.

Chambers, the baby is fine. Everything related to the pregnancy is excellent, but the tests show you have early signs of leukemia.'

"Even though tired, Babe was the strongest of us all. This sickness helped us get closer and closer."

Ray stopped for a moment. "When we knew the end was near, Babe helped me get ready for her being gone.

"Babe would say, 'Ray, this is Daddy's plan. We have had a great life together these sixteen years. And these last three years, because of the Wednesday/Saturday—Love of Union—question, have been the best. We've spent a lot of really quality time together.'

"'And we will have an eternity together soon. Please remember that! Be sure to remind the kids regularly, especially the little one how much I love them.'"

Ray stopped again—this time with a tear.

"She wanted to live till Mother's Day. She did, even feeling good with visitors that day.

"It's like she said, 'Thanks, Daddy for letting me live through Mother's Day; I'm ready to come home now!'

"She went home to live with her Divine Daddy at 3:17 am the Monday after Mother's Day. The baby was just 19 months old."

Ray stopped again. Then with a smile, he said, "Babe was right. Daddy, her favorite name for God, would take care of us. My older sister never married. She stepped right in to raise the kids—she was a wonderful help to me and a second mother to the kids.

"Looking back, three things come to mind. Babe's two facts are so right. First, every moment is a gift. Secondly, we never know how many more moments we will be given.

"The third thing that comes to mind is, what Bill told you is right. These two facts helped us take the Wednesday/Saturday question, *How can I be closer to and more united with Babe today,* to new heights.

"If, when we met Bill and Carrie, I knew Babe and I only had three more years together, I would have wanted to live those three years exactly the same way—*being closer to and more united with Babe each day."*

As Maria drove home, John captured Ray's insights with some feeling, especially adapted to Maria and himself living life to the fullest NOW.

Maria and John's Visitation Schedule

Your Goal: *To discover a quick to learn, easy to use, proven to work path to grow your true love daily.*

Monday Appointment

Love begins *When you know, value, and appreciate the other person.* Visit with Pat and Harry
The 'I got ya game' was leading to divorce. The True Love That Lasts questions saved their marriage; their three children living with two parents.

Monday and Thursday Question
How can I appreciate and value the one I love more today?

Tuesday Appointment

Love of Benevolence: *You wish for and do good for the one you love.* Visit with Joan and Dan
The questions work even when just Joan asked them. Dan benefits but Joan feels the benefits most. 3 of 3 vs. 2 for 3.

Tuesday and Friday Question
How can I please and surprise the one I love more today?

Wednesday Appointment

Love of Union: *You want to be closer to and united with the one you love.* Visit with Ray
Ray said the Love of Union question helped him and Babe be much closer and made wonderful the three years before she went home to God.

Wednesday and Saturday Question
How can I be closer to and united with the one I love more today?

Coaches: Carrie & Bill, honored to be called "***The Young Couple***"

Critical Insights to Remember

The Crowning Glory, the Apex of Love is *Union with the beloved.*

Babe's Two Facts

1. *My life especially this moment is a gift from mom, dad, and Daddy.*

2. *We have this moment. Use it! We don't know how many next moments we will have!*

Key Insight for Maria and John

Whether we have 55 more moments or 55+ years, we're smartest to celebrate life NOW by living each moment and learning to love to the fullest.

CHAPTER 12

The Easy Way to Grow the True Love That Lasts Habit

The next evening John and Maria went back to report all they had learned to Bill and Carrie. With great excitement they shared how Pat and Harry Dolesh had changed the *I got ya* slippery road to divorce to the path to a Crystal Marriage using the start of love question—*how can I value and appreciate my spouse more today*?

They summarized the benefits Joan Jackson reported she and her husband both receive, even though only she uses the True Love That Lasts questions, especially the Love of Benevolence question—*how can I please and surprise my spouse today?*

Finally, they spoke of the benefits Ray Chambers cherished because he used the Love of Union question—*how can I be closer to and more united with my spouse today*? He said if he knew he only had three more years to be with Babe, he would have wanted to live them exactly the way they did—closer because of the Love of Union question.

John shared his detailed notes and received a much appreciated 'brilliant' from Bill for taking notes and capturing the important insights.

Bill and Carrie made it even more exciting and meaningful for John and Maria by listening very attentively and asking appropriate questions.

Finally, Bill guided their focus. "Looking back for the moment from the proposal at Starbucks, your search for a secret, and now your three visits, what one thing stands out most in your minds?"

Both John and Maria thought for a moment.

John eventually replied, "I was very concerned that the questions would be too demanding. We still need to find out what that fourth question is. I wondered if we could meet Maria's goal; were the questions quick to learn, easy to use, and have the proven power to grow our love a little each day?

"I listened very closely to each of the three sets of people we visited; they didn't seem to have any trouble making the first three questions a part of their daily lives. And I also like the total freedom to answer each of the questions in any way appropriate at the time."

Turning to Bill, John continued, "Each time you said they were *so very simple,* I hoped you were right, but had my doubts. I'm happy to say, doubts are gone!"

"Thanks, John," Bill replied. "I'm glad you checked that very closely with each interview." He then turned and asked, "Maria, what one thing stands out for you?"

Maria replied, "I agree with John. We discussed the simplicity of the question of the day each evening after the visits. But the number one thing I'm concerned about is growing the habit and avoiding divorce. If we get married—and I haven't said 'Yes' yet—and have the family we want, we'll still have to be concerned about our careers, our kids' education, our finances, etc.

"I want True Love That Lasts. I still ask, 'Can we build the True Love That Lasts habit, so this becomes a lifelong path using *Kaizen* to grow our love a little each day?'"

Carrie now hopped in. "Maria, that is an excellent insight and concern! Coaching many couples, we discovered focusing on growing a habit is critical. Bill will share with you the True Love That Lasts Habit Builder."

Bill replied, "The insight for this very powerful habit builder comes from a very unlikely source, a famous comedian. The story begins when this comedian was a struggling newcomer. He had the reputation of coming up with a good joke every three or four days. But that was not enough to build his career on. He was told that to be successful, he needed to work on creating jokes at least 30 minutes a day. But he found it hard to get himself to do that.

"Eventually, he hit upon a habit builder. He made himself a promise that he would work on creating jokes at least 30 minutes a day. To make certain he did it, he kept track on a calendar. He had two simple rules:

- cross off the day even if you just do a little
- don't break the streak.

"It worked! Some days his jokes were terrible. But by building the habit, he eventually created enough jokes about ordinary things that he got a TV show—funny things about very ordinary everyday happenings. After ten seasons he retired, rumored to be worth over $100,000,000.

"To save you time, I've created a calendar that you can adapt to the uniqueness of your situation. I've also added the three rules that make it work with the True Love That Lasts questions and your goal. Review it and then ask any questions."

He handed them the True Love That Lasts Habit Builder.

The True Love That Lasts Habit Builder

1. Put the questions on a calendar where you begin your day. **2.** When you have asked and answered the question of the day, cross off the day. **3.** Don't break the streak. ***Option***: *Add a word or phrase related to your discovery or action each day.*

Monday/Thursday: How can I appreciate and value the one I love more today?
Tuesday/Friday: How can I please and surprise the one I love more today?
Wednesday/Saturday: How can I be closer to and united with the one I love more today?

Goal: A quick to learn, easy to use, proven to work lifelong path to help us grow our love and relationship a little each day.

Expected Benefits: **Each day** we will enjoy our love growing a little. On each anniversary, especially **our 55+,** we will be much closer than we are today. We will be enjoying a **Crystal Marriage.**

Sunday	Monday	Tuesday	Wednesday	Thursday	Friday	Saturday

After reviewing the entire calendar, John asked, "What are the little lines for in the upper corner of each box?"

Bill replied, "This calendar covers a month. You can make copies of it for any month. Those lines are to put in the dates of the month."

Maria asked, "Do we need to share our answers with our partner?"

Carrie replied, "Very important question. Here is where the freedom of the Secret of Growing True Love That Lasts comes in. The answer is: only when you want to.

"I find that, at times, I want to share my answers with Bill. At times, sharing stifles my creativity, so I don't share. In so many ways, the Secret of Growing True Love That Lasts stands for freedom that encourages creativity."

Bill added, "Another point of freedom is keeping a record of your answers. I find it useful for me to put a word or two related to the answer I come up with each day.

"I recommend it. It helps me be more aware of the question of the day all day long; thus, the question of the day becomes a large event and has a greater impact.

"And reviewing the record of the last couple weeks or months inspires me for today."

Carrie added with a smile, "I only do that when I have a brilliant answer." They all laughed.

Bill then made one request. "I'd like to make one very important suggestion. I find those who put the calendar in a place where they see it first thing in the morning are *most successful*. I have mine where I have my first cup of coffee and meditate in the morning. I rarely miss a day."

Bill continued, "Where you locate your calendar is so simple and so important to build the habit, I'd like to ask you to commit now to put it there when you start tomorrow morning."

John replied, "Seems simple enough. However, I might just use the question of the day today."

Bill replied, "That's even better."

Carrie ended the visit with, "Call us anytime with any questions. We look forward to seeing you back here a month and a day from today. We also look forward to hearing your success stories.

"We'll plan to share with you the problems we were experiencing as we were preparing to celebrate our tenth anniversary. It was solving those problems that helped us take the Secret of Growing True Love That Lasts to new, even Divine, heights."

John, ever the one interested in ALL four questions asked, "And then we will learn the fourth question?"

Carrie grinned, "The fourth question was born in the problems we had when preparing to celebrate our tenth anniversary. Yes, John, you'll definitely learn the fourth question; why it is needed; how well it works; and how it guided us to take the Secret of Growing True Love That Lasts to new, even Divine heights."

With that, Maria and John were off for a month of discovery.

After they left, Bill asked Carrie, "Will there be enough immediate benefits in using the question of the day to convince John—and especially Maria—it could help them focus and grow their love a little each day for a lifetime?"

Carrie added, "Will it be enough for Maria to say 'Yes' to John's proposal?"

Both Carrie and Bill looked forward to John and Maria's return in a month and a day.

CHAPTER 13

Were the Discoveries of the First Month Enough?

When John and Maria arrived smiling a month later, Carrie was the first to notice. "Maria, I see a ring! Congratulations. Tell us about it!"

The excited look on Carrie's face was exactly what Maria was looking forward to. Maria began, "The month did not turn out as I expected. Bill, something you explained I didn't much understand at the time and certainly didn't think important, turned out to be the turning point."

Bill replied, "Please tell us about it."

Maria continued, "When you explained that to become a crystal like a diamond, an event is needed. With carbon, the event of great pressure forces the molecules into an orderly formation; and that event produces a crystal that is a diamond from what might have been just coal. As I said, when you explained it, I could not foresee how that applied to me and my saying 'Yes' to John's proposal.

"Asking the question of the day turned out to be more than affecting that moment. It was like an event or a process that influenced my entire day. Like the pressure gave carbon the special powers to become a crystal diamond, the question of the day gave me more special powers all day. It aligned all my thoughts into orderly patterns related to John and me. The question of the day was guiding me to grow the True Love I wanted and convincing me it would last."

With great excitement, Maria continued, "First, I discovered all day things I valued and appreciated in John."

John, who could not hold himself back, immediately said, "I really like this!"

With a broad smile Maria continued, "I also noticed when he shared with me some of the increased values, he appreciates in me, like crystal, he makes me shine. As a result, I wanted to shine even brighter for him because he recognized my thoughtfulness and many other little things I did for him, even things I did automatically.

"I think the *biggest thing* the question of the day gave me day after day was to see that Deming's *Kaizen*—continuous improvement—and our version—*a little more love each day*—was working. My thought patterns were being organized daily by the question of the day to look for things to appreciate in John, or to discover how to surprise and please him. Or, most of all, how to be closer to and more united to John.

"And talking with John, I could see the event of his asking the question of the day having a similar result. So, at the end of the third week, I told John if he would meet me at Starbucks that Saturday night at 10:13 p.m. and offer me a ring, I'd accept it with real pride.

"He did, and here it is." She again held up her ring. It seemed to sparkle with extra brilliance. And if there was any doubt, the smile on her face was overwhelming proof.

John completed the presentation with, "I was and am thrilled."

Carrie added, "Bill and I are both thrilled. Maria, you deserve a 'brilliant' for that explanation of how the daily event of asking the True Love That Lasts question was leading you to be convinced that you and John could grow a Crystal Marriage. My psychology teacher would be proud of you."

Maria added, "Let me add one more thing. Bill talked of the self that gets up in the morning—the get-going self or the reflective self. I must say that before this I was definitely a get-going self.

"The event or process of asking the question of the day, then meditating on my answer, is certainly moving me to let more of my reflective-self shine.

"John, thanks for letting me tell my story. Now I'm sure Bill and Carrie would like to hear your story and the list you prepared."

John continued as the orderly person he was. "Last night Maria and I were discussing the excitement of seeing you today. I made a list of five things I especially wanted to share with you.

1. Breaking the chain
2. Keeping a record
3. Knowing Maria is asking the question of the day
4. The Doleshes' *I got ya* game and divorce
5. The Freedom of the Crystal Marriage"

Bill replied, "That is quite a list. Let's hear each."

1. Breaking the chain.

"The first week, I broke the chain because I didn't follow your suggestion and live up to my commitment of putting the calendar and score card where I had my first cup of coffee. A bit embarrassed, when I followed your suggestion and put it where I begin my day, I haven't missed a day since."

2. Keeping a record.

"I started to record the discovery or action of the day by setting my cell for 10:13 p.m. I haven't missed a night since. This simple record helps me make the event of answering the question of the day easier to remember and more powerful. Most importantly, I found out that committing to a short recording each night makes me more *accountable to myself.*

"Answering the question of the day is not just a one–minute event. As Maria explained, it becomes an all-day event or process that very easily orders my thoughts that grows our love and our relationship."

3. Knowing Maria is asking the question of the day

"I really like the fact that she is looking for things in me to appreciate. Two things happen. First, it makes it much easier for me to ask and answer the question of the day. Secondly, I especially appreciate some of her surprises. She has gone from the cooking repertoire of two things—boiling water and making coffee—to the ability to make lasagna; she now has a cooking repertoire of three."

That brought a love hit from Maria. Undaunted, John repeated, "Honey, I really do love your lasagna."

4. The Doleshes' I got ya game and divorce

"I became aware I play the *I got ya* game with my older brother. And it is having a very negative effect. The 'divorce' with my brother is looking like *never talking again*. I'm a bit ashamed of this. I'm committed to change this never–talk–again situation. For my brother, I changed the question of the day to the question-of-the-week."

5. The Flexibility of the True Love that Lasts process

"The surprise/please question of Friday has become our Saturday question because of tennis and racquet ball on Friday night."

At the end of the discussion, John asked, "In these short four weeks, we could easily find new things to appreciate in each other. But don't you run out of things after some months, or even years? A serious problem."

John was surprised when both Carrie and Bill laughed.

Carrie answered, "As I shared before, we rarely if ever experience that. We did have some problems as we were getting closer to our tenth anniversary, which Bill will tell you about in a minute. Bill, share with them your backstop question if you ever did not come up with an easy answer."

Bill gladly replied, "On the very few occasions when it happens, I just ask myself, 'What would I miss most if Carrie was not here?' The answer is motivating. Also, I learned that valuable lesson from Babe Chambers. As Ray probably told you, Babe helped Carrie and me take the Love of Union to new heights by learning to live life to the fullest each moment. She helped us realize that each moment is a gift and—what is most important—the number of *gifts has a limit.* We're motivated to be close now because we don't know how many more moments—how many more gifts of a moment—we will have.

"This is easier for us—married 55 years—to say. But to whom does this not apply? We have experienced couples much younger than us run out of the gift of the next moment. Earlier today I discovered a former colleague more than twenty years younger than I ran out of moments—hit by a pickup truck.

"We are delighted with your progress. Now, I think it's time to share with you our problems as our tenth anniversary was approaching and the wonderful things we discovered coming out of those challenges that made our Crystal Marriage so much better for the last 45+ years."

Chapter 14

The Fourth Question: What Is the Skill Many Lack?

Carrie began, "As we were getting ready to celebrate our tenth anniversary, a lot of things were great. But Bill and I both felt something was missing, something significant!"

Bill picked up the thought, "Carrie is right on. Something significant, and maybe more than one thing. But what?"

Carrie continued, "After much thought, with so many things going so well, we feared we had begun to take each other for granted. Maria, when you first presented your concerns about taking each other for granted, I said to myself, 'That is very insightful,' remembering our tenth anniversary."

Maria felt good that Carrie remembered and appreciated her concern of taking each other for granted over time.

Bill explained, "We didn't want just a party. Carrie and I agreed that we needed a celebration that would help us get back on track to build our relationship and grow our love daily. Carrie suggested a tenth anniversary honeymoon. I suggested a retreat together. With so many things going on and three kids, as usual, money was tight. We couldn't do both."

Bill pointed out, "Then the invitation to our tenth reunion arrived. The topics our departments would present seemed designed just for us."

Carrie agreed, "Bill is right. My dissertation director, Professor Simons, was going to present: *'Optimizing Marital Relationships: Being willing to share who you really are and accepting who your partner really is.'* That caught my attention.

"However, in the details there was this one line that made me feel we had to go: *'the skill most people lack*: the ability to share what they REALLY like, don't like and want from their partner.'

"The phrase *'...the skill most people lack'* rang true for us. Bill and I were too busy to even consider what we really liked, didn't like, and wanted from each other."

Bill added, "Carrie convinced me we should bite the financial bullet and go. I didn't need much convincing when I considered what my favorite professor, Professor Reed, was going to present: *'Who Has a Vested Interest in Your Marital Success?'*

"I was interested. Like Carrie, the description of the talk made me more interested. 'If your parents are dead and you have no children, there are still *at least three very important parties* who have a vested interest in your marriage succeeding. Who are the three? Come and see!' That was so Prof. Reed, building curiosity. Carrie and I were two. I could not imagine who the third was. We hoped it might give us insight into our vague problems.

"Reed was our favorite because, as you might remember, my Theology department and Carrie's Psychology department didn't see eye–to–eye related to our single dissertation on True Love. It was Professor Reed who brought success out of chaos. With his guidance, the two departments even said they learned a lot.

"Also, very important, it was Professor Reed who helped us adapt the True Love of our dissertation to find the simple power to grow our True Love daily, i.e. *ask the right question at the right time* that the True Love That Lasts questions are built on. Maybe he could help us discover what we were missing now.

"Because of these two talks, we absolutely had to go.

"After we signed up, Carrie suggested we make it a special point to spend some time with Professor Reed privately. So, we made an appointment with him just after his presentation."

Carrie outlined the next steps. "Bill and I agreed, today we will first share what we learned from my psychology professor and how question four of the Secret came about. Then we will share with you how his theology professor helped us take the True Love That Lasts questions to a more realistic, even higher level.

"It has been using the Secret of Growing True Love That Lasts at this, more realistic higher level, that has worked so well for us for the forty-five years since our tenth anniversary. It earned us *'Still The Young Couple'* on our fiftieth fifth anniversary cake."

Bill began. "Our first 'Aha' was Carrie's professor's pointing out the difference between the Golden Rule and the Platinum Rule. The Golden Rule that we all know so well is: *Do unto others as you would have others do unto to you.*

"In the Platinum Rule I find an insightful, even brilliant variation," he said, smiling at John when he said brilliant. "It is, *Do unto others as others would have you do unto them.* We immediately realized that each of our True Love That Lasts questions followed the Golden Rule—excellent in themselves. It pointed out a problem; we were missing a very important part.

"I was always asking myself how I can appreciate, surprise or be closer to Carrie. We needed something so Carrie could tell me what she wanted or needed from me and vice versa."

Bill continued, "Carrie's professor went on to explain—*a skill most people lack* is the ability to tell their partner what they want or need from them. And do it in such a way that it does not damage the relationship by driving the other person away, but actually promotes the relationship.

"When Carrie's professor explained her **Fact–Feeling–Request Process**, it seemed like exactly what we needed.

"The professor pointed out two things. First, partners rarely take time to tell each other what they really want from each other, *except when they are disappointed and angry.* To angrily tell your partner what you want but don't get, at times indicates you expect them to read your mind. This can harm the relationship.

"Second, many people hesitate to tell their partner what they really want because *they don't know how* to do it in a way that avoids an argument and promotes discussion; i.e. discussion that does not destroy the relationship, but improves it. The professor's simple Fact–Feeling–Request Process takes care of both problems."

Bill added, "As the name suggests, you begin with something that you both can accept as *fact*. Then you share your *feelings* about that fact. Here you are sharing your true self. It could be a feeling that you are not proud of. But it's your true self.

"Feelings are rarely a point of discussion and more a sharing of your true self. For example: if someone says, 'when you did X, I really got excited;' it would be rare for the other person to say, 'Oh! No, you didn't get excited.'

"This also holds for a negative example. If someone says, 'When you did Y, I was really disappointed;' it would be unlikely that the other would reply, 'When I did Y, you weren't disappointed.'

"The professor pointed out that sharing feelings is actually sharing who a person really is—their true self.

"Finally—and here is where asking the right question at the right time comes in—you ask a question in the form of a request. Here is the relationship building power. You invite your partner to tell you what they can or will do about your request."

Maria asked, "Can you help us understand with some examples?"

Bill replied, "Here is one I might use next Sunday that will demonstrate the simplicity and usefulness of the process.

"Carrie,

1. **FACT**
   When you make your chicken with broccoli soup,

2. **FEELING**
   I really love it.

3. **REQUEST**
   Could we have that more often, like once a week?"

Carrie, with a huge smile, "Clever, Bill! Sure, we can do it. But once a week might be too often. But more often is doable."

"Great!" Bill immediately replied. "You see the Fact–Feeling–Request works. Carrie gets a chance to reply and she knows the real me certainly likes her chicken with broccoli soup."

Carrie responded, "Bill, since you shared a positive example from real life, let me share a real–life one, but a bit negative."

Maria requested, "Carrie, it would help me with this example if you would show us what might happen without the process first and then what happens with the Fact-Feeling-Request Process."

Carrie replied, "Certainly. And we can go back to the *I got ya game* Pat and Harry Dolesh were playing that took them toward a devastating divorce. They were the first couple you visited.

"Bill has a new Prius. You just need to have the key in your pocket to start the car. And to stop the engine, you don't take out the key—which is in your pocket—you just press the start/stop button. Bill finds it hard to remember to turn the car off.

"I could have said, with some negative feeling, 'Bill that's the fourth time this week you forgot to turn the car off. With the car still running, it could get stolen or roll out and kill someone. *You never learn*!' And he could rightly feel, I'm putting him down."

Bill retorted, "If we were playing the Doleshes' *I got ya game,* I might have said, 'Let's talk about your leaving the light on in your office. I have turned it out for you at least five times in just this last week, costing money! *You never learn! Got ya*."

Carrie then summed things up. "This *I got ya game* could end up with no one winning and our relationship of trust and caring for each other being the loser."

Carrie continued, "Now let me use the Fact-Feeling-Request to show you the difference—how it can build the relationship of trust and caring.

"Bill,

1. **FACT**
   When you get out of your car without turning it off,

2. **FEELING**
   I really get worried that all kinds of negative things can happen. Like the running car could be stolen.

3. **REQUEST**
   Could you figure out a way to break that bad habit?"

Bill—slightly blushing—"I agree with you. Do you have a suggestion to help me?"

Carrie gladly replied smiling, "A significant donation to my crochet fund each time you forget might help you break the habit quickly. And the bigger the agreed donation, the quicker you'll break the habit."

With John and Maria smiling about *the bigger the agreed donation,* Bill good naturedly added, "Agreed, amount to be discussed."

John, listening and taking notes, asked, "When do you use this Fact–Feeling–Request process?"

Bill responded, "A very good question..."

And before he could complete his sentence, John smiling asked, "Not brilliant?"

Bill laughed and shot back, "Not clearly brilliant. However, if you can use this once each Sunday, and then at other times that seem appropriate, and this helps you earn 'Still *The Young Couple'* on your fiftieth–fifth anniversary cake, I'll have to say 'brilliant.'"

When the laughter stopped, Maria, quiet for a long time, interjected, "First, I want to say I'm glad you pointed out that, by your tenth anniversary, you were starting to take each other for granted. I want to say also, I see the value of using the Fact-Feeling-Request Process each Sunday to either show your appreciation or get something you really want or need.

"What about an example of use during the week?"

Bill jumped in. "I have one I used yesterday. Carrie lost her dog three years ago. And she is very interested in getting another but hesitates because it would stop us from travelling as much as we would like. But I know that we can find some of our kids to take the dog when we go. Yesterday, she again showed me some dogs she likes on the internet. I said:

"Carrie,

1. **FACT**
   When you review puppies on the internet,

2. **FEELING**
   I'm thrilled because you always seem to enjoy it so much.

3. **REQUEST**
   I hope you will keep it up and get a puppy when we come back from our next trip.

Carrie replied, "That's right. You did say that, and I didn't even notice the format. I did enjoy the hug you gave me at the time, but I'm still not sure about getting a puppy."

Bill laughed, "I understand what that means. She is saying 'I'll get one as soon as you talk me into it.'" The other three laughed.

Maria added, "So you can use the Fact-Feeling-Request anytime. But you do it at least each Sunday to keep sharing your real self and what you really like/want from your partner."

Carrie now added, "While I get some refreshments. John, why don't you complete your notes. After the refreshments are served, Bill can share what our favorite Professor Reed presented: *Who has a Vested Interest in Your Marital Success?"*

Forever and Ever
...And Then Some

The Sunday and When Needed Question

Fact–Feeling–Request Process

FACT: *State a fact–hopefully you both agree it is a fact, avoiding disagreement.*

FEELING: *Your feeling when the fact happens. It is hard to disagree with feelings. When truthful, it is a fact that you feel that way.*

REQUEST: *What you would like the other to do. (This is the fourth question and the source of power to build the relationship.)*

- **Give the other time to respond.**
- **Come to an agreement on action(s) to be taken.**

WHEN Can This Be Used?

- **At least once each Sunday to reveal more and more of your true self; what you like /want from your partner**
- **And any time it is appropriate.**

Benefits to be Expected

1. *You share your true self when sharing what you want, like, need and when sharing your feelings.*
2. *You get more of what you want/need and build the relationship on truth in the process.*

Chapter 15

Will You Let Me Love You—Now?

Bill started, "As I shared earlier, in the description of Professor Reed's talk, it said: 'If your parents have gone home to God and you have no children, there are still at least three parties who have a vested interest in your marital success. *Who are these three?* Come and see!'

"If Carrie and I are the first two parties, the only third party we could think of was the government. Was that what Reed—the outstanding theology professor—hinted at?

"As I said, we hoped his talk would give us more insights into the vague marital problems we were feeling.

"He opened up with two intriguing questions:

1. **Did you earn your existence?**

2. **What was the intent of your source?**

Bill continued, "Professor Reed was and is great at two things:

- sticking to the facts and

- arriving at hard-to-dispute conclusions.

"He answered the first question with two facts and a conclusion.

Fact: There was a time when each of you was not!

Fact: Totally because of the gratuitous goodness of God and the love of your parents, today here you are.

Conclusion: You did not in any way earn your existence."

Bill continued the explanation, "Building on this, he proceeded to answer his second question, 'What was the intent of your source?'

"He first focused on our parents and their intent in having us. Again, asking the right question at the right time: was it your parents' intent to love each other, have you, and then say: 'Hello, goodbye, good luck?'

"Or, was it to have you, bless you in as many ways as possible while they raise you, and enjoy a relationship with you for the rest of their lives? With a few exceptions, the obvious answer is the latter.

"The Professor then pointed to a happening from his life that emphatically demonstrated the fact that parents want to have a lasting relationship with their children. In the last couple years, four of his friends have left his area and moved hundreds of miles away to facilitate continuing to grow and enjoy their relationships with their children and grandchildren.

"Professor Reed then turned his attention to God.

"Did God want to create you and say, 'Goodbye, good luck' or was it to create you and build a relationship with you here in this life as He guides you to an even greater life for all eternity?

"The Professor pointed out that the answer to the question about our parents' intent is obvious to most. Unfortunately, the answer to the part about God's intent is not so obvious to some.

"Then the professor pointed out the first of three WOW Take–Home Values. Because most of the alumni were married, he especially tailored it to us."

WOW Take–Home Values from the Professor's Presentation

1. **God—our Source—has a *vested interest* in our success, especially our *marital success.***

2.

3.

"The Professor continued to answer his question, 'What was the intent of our source?' by first reviewing the nature of God and then True Love.

"To help understand the nature of God, he first quoted St. John's first letter, 'God is love!'

"Then he quoted the beginning of the Old Testament, 'Love the Lord your God with all your heart and with all your soul and with all your strength.'

"He pointed out that these quotes and many others in the bible clearly demonstrate that it is God's very nature to love. As our source, He created us because He loves us and—as is nature to all love—wants to be loved in return."

At this, John demonstrated that he was understanding by remarking, "That is something that I don't think you mentioned before—it is part of the very nature of love to want to be loved in return."

"Brilliant, John!" Bill replied. "You're exactly correct. When the professor said this, it was an Aha for me. I think we skipped or did not emphasize the desire to be loved in return in our dissertation on the working definition of True Love.

"Here the Professor was pointing out that even—or especially—God wants to be loved in return.

"Speaking of our dissertation, the Professor surprised and honored us by quoting from it to begin his explanation of the dilemma God was facing when he created us. He began:

"*True Love begins* when you know, value, and appreciate someone.

"Then True Love grows in two directions simultaneously:

- *The Love of Benevolence*—wishing good for and doing good for the one you love.

- *The Love of Union*—wanting to be closer to and united with the one you love.

"The Professor then pointed out that for True Love to begin and then grow, the person must be free. The person loving must:

- *freely* value and appreciate the one loved

- *freely* wish good for and do good for the one loved

- *freely* want to be closer to and united with the one loved

"Here was God's dilemma. He knew that to be Truly Loved in return, the person needs to be free for each of the three parts of love to function correctly.

"However, when He creates billions of people, some—even a few—might say NO! to returning his love. So what was he to do?

"The Professor then reviewed God's love using the way we defined the operational definition of love in our dissertation.

The Beginning of Love

"True Love begins when you know, value, and appreciate someone.

"God had you and me in His mind—He knew us—before He created us. Because He *values* and *appreciates* you and me, He created us.

"But before He began creating people, He had to make a decision:

- make them so they *can't say NO*! to his love?

or

- make them *free to say NO!* to his love?

"Here the Professor's sense of humor came out. He pointed out that God is not only infinite, at times, He is an infinite gambler. So God makes a gamble.

"God values our *freely given love* so much He risks our saying *NO to His love.*

"This impressed us so much it became our second Wow Take–Home Value."

WOW Take–Home Values from the Professor's Presentation

1. God has a *vested interest* in our success, especially our *marital success.*

2. **God values our *freely given love* so much, He risks our saying *NO to His love.***

3.

The Love of Benevolence

"The Professor explained God has an ace in the hole. He figures if He overwhelms us with His love and blessings, it will be hard for anyone to say 'No!' to returning his infinite love.

"The Professor pointed out that the bible shows us how God loves us in so many ways. He understands that we more or less are aware of what the bible tells us of God's love.

"But what most people are not aware of is how modern science shows us an unlimited number of ways God loves us. The Professor inspired us with his top four.

1. The Big Bang

"In 1962, Arno Penzias and Robert Wilson of Bell Labs discovered evidence that the universe was created about 13.5 billion years ago. Because God wanted that personal love relationship with each of us, he created a universe for us and started the process of preparing it for us to live in.

2. DNA

"On February 21, 1953 Francis Crick and James Watson discovered DNA. Science has since proven that all living things going back 4.3 billion years are guided in their development by DNA. Our DNA does three things:

- It guides our development.
- It connects us to our parents since half of our DNA comes from each parent.

• It makes each of us a unique individual that God loves and wants to be loved by in return.

3. Energy

"Most of us came to our tenth reunion using a car in some way. The Professor pointed out that 900 million years ago, God was thoughtful enough to have the vegetation grow, die, and become pressed into oil so that our gas-powered cars could bring us to this tenth reunion. Each time we drive a car we might thank God for His foresight and thoughtfulness of 900 million years ago.

4. Oxygen—The Most Impressive

"The Professor then stopped for a moment. When he had all our undivided attention, he said, 'In a moment I am going to say, *Breathe deeply.* I want you to take a deep breath. Then I will count to ten. During my count, I want you to imagine where science says the oxygen you are enjoying came from and who makes it a gift to you in this moment.'

"After he said, *Breathe deeply* and counted to ten, he pointed out two amazing facts from science. First, science tells us, in the Big Bang all atoms were either hydrogen or helium. No oxygen! To get oxygen and the heavier metals like iron, you needed the tremendous heat you could get only in the explosion of a supernova.

"The oxygen you are now enjoying is a gift from your thoughtful God, loving you five or ten billion years ago when He arranged for a supernova to explode. The intense heat of the supernova exploding created the oxygen we are now enjoying as His gift.

"The second amazing fact the Professor explained was that each, especially this, moment is a gift of our all loving God so we can live life to the fullest this moment."

At that, John—still feeling good about the 'Brilliant' Bill gave him a little while ago—jumped in. "That reminds me a bit of what Babe taught you many years later about living life to the fullest.

"This moment and each moment are gifts. Not everyone like her younger sister and daughter enjoyed the many moments that we enjoy."

Bill replied with enthusiasm, "Brilliant again, John. You are right! Babe's sharing came many years later. She focused on living life to the fullest, partly motivated by the fact that each moment is a gift that her younger sister and first daughter only enjoyed too few of."

Maria—ever the insightful one—added, "You know, it strikes me that everyone living enjoys this moment and the oxygen we breath in common.

"But those who see it as a freely given gift from God are so much richer. They can be so much happier when they appreciate it as a gift from their Source. It reminds me of G.K. Chesterton's insight, 'The beginning of happiness is gratitude.' In this case gratitude for each of our NOWs and the oxygen we enjoy making the NOWs continue."

Bill, now really delighted, replied, "Maria and John, a double brilliant. Also, a great introduction to the Love of Union and the third *WOW Take–Home Value* which, as you will shortly see, is GOD'S QUESTION—an ace in the hole to encourage us to love Him.

The Love of Union

"As we've said, love begins when you know, value, and appreciate someone. The Professor explained that precisely because you value and appreciate the one you love so much, you want to be with them. This naturally leads to the Love of Union, the apex or climax of love.

"The Love of Union—wanting to be closer to and united with the one you love.

"The same is true for God. Because he values and appreciates us so much—after all He created us—He wants to be with us. But here again is His great dilemma. Because He loves us, He has given us all we have, including life this moment.

"However, He also has given us our freedom. If He forces us to love Him, He can't have the freely returned True Love relationship with us He wants.

"What is He to do? How can he solve this dilemma?

"It is as if He says, because I love you so much just as you are with all your shortcomings, I will continue to give you your freedom this moment—this NOW. And I will honor your freedom.

"Honoring your freedom, I will ask you to let me love you. It is as if He is saying:

'I value you just as you are,

I honor your freedom, Will you let me love you—NOW?'

"This is the third *WOW Take–Home Value,* one of God's most powerful aces in the hole, the *invitation to let Him love us NOW even with all our warts and shortcomings!"*

Forever and Ever
...And Then Some

WOW Take–Home Values from the Professor's Presentation

1. God has a *vested interest* in our success, especially our *marital success.*

2. God values our *freely given love* so much, He risks our saying *NO to His love.*

3. **It is as if He is saying:**

   "I value you just as you are,

   I honor your freedom,

   Will you let me love you—NOW?"

After Bill presented the three WOW Take–Home Values, there was a thoughtful silence.

Carrie then quietly broke the hush with, "Bill is right. These were life-changing Take–Home Values.

"I especially remember the Professor's words as if God was talking, 'Just as you are this moment.' For me the Professor was saying for God, with all my warts and shortcomings—that God knows perfectly—he wants me to let Him love me NOW.

"Ever since the Professor's presentation some 45+ years ago, several times a day I pause, take a deep breath, and think:

- God has given me another moment, a wonderful NOW.
- Then I can hear the Professor asking for God:

"I value you just as you are.
I honor your freedom,
Will you let me love you—NOW?"

There was another pause.

Quietly Carrie continued, "The Professor pointed out it is as if God is saying, 'I want you exactly as you are this moment.' This encourages me, no matter how I feel I messed up, that God still wants to love me.

"I try to respond to His question with a *Strong Yes!* and then get totally involved in how I am trying to serve Him that moment.

"To our surprise, when we met with the Professor after his talk, he even had more positive news that helped us understand the intent our of source better.

"I think Bill wants to tell that story."

Chapter 16

We Came With A Vague Problem We Left With A Divine Partner

Bill gladly jumped back in, "Getting back to end of the Professor's presentation, we were certainly on a high note. We were thrilled and honored that he used the working definitions of True Love from our dissertation. We were wowed by his three Take–Home Values.

"However, we still had a serious challenge. It was obvious in our first ten years of marriage we asked the True Love That Lasts questions alone.

"We had not even the slightest idea that God might be interested in helping us, let along His having a vested interest in our success, especially our marital success.

"Now, we had a potential partner because of God's vested interest—as the Professor explained.

"The problem I was feeling was how do we make that *potential partnership* with God related to our marital success an *actual partnership*?

"I didn't have the foggiest idea of how to start!

"Luckily, because Professor Reed had been so helpful when we were students—especially helping us with our dissertation—before we came to the reunion, we lined up a personal visit scheduled shortly after his presentation.

"We hoped to get the advantage of his advice and experience to make that potential partnership with God an actual one related to our marital success.

"Professor Reed was so glad to see us. After we chatted a bit to catch up, we shared with him in great detail the uneasiness we were feeling as we approached our tenth wedding anniversary.

"We both had this vague feeling something was missing in our marriage—and how the two presentations seemed created just for us.

"I then asked him for *practical suggestions* to implement his insight that God had a vested interest in our marital success as we used the True Love That Lasts questions.

"He said he was so glad to see us because of the experiences he has had related to the True Love That Lasts questions in the past few years.

"He wanted to share with us those experiences and thought they pointed to the implementation suggestions I was asking for.

"He began by saying that in the years after we graduated, every time he heard of an alumni couple who met, married at the university, and subsequently got divorced, he asked himself, 'I wonder if they had used the True Love That Lasts questions, would they have avoided divorce. Would they now be enjoying a successful marriage and a much more fulfilling life?'

"About five years ago it seemed to him that the number of divorces was increasing. He needed to do something about it. But what?

"He thought of sharing the True Love That Lasts questions with his theology classes. But he hesitated because the class would ask him what effect or influence the questions had on him and his marriage. He didn't want to say he didn't use them. So, he decided if he wanted to share them with future classes, he needed to have a personal experience of the questions, how they worked, and the expected benefits.

"After some thought, he decided that he would ask the questions himself first without telling his wife. Doing it this way would help him avoid an objection and give him a benefit.

"The objection he anticipated was some of the class might push back trying the questions saying that for the questions to work, both partners have to ask them. It would not work in their case because they were sure their partner would not want to use the questions.

"The benefit it would give him was related. If he could make them work with just his asking them, the True Love That Lasts questions would be more useful and flexible."

John then asked, "So what happened. Did it work? Did his wife ever discover what he was doing?"

At this point, Carrie answered, "John, I had the same question when we met with the Professor. Because we knew the Professor so well, I asked him exactly that.

"He turned to me with a big smile and said, 'After about six months, my wife made a comment one evening that I seemed to be more loving lately. Was I hiding something, or wanted something?'

"At this we laughed. He told her that he felt their relationship was growing. He explained the entire situation to her and invited her to begin asking the daily questions about him. She accepted and things got even better.

"He said this made sharing with his students even easier and more compelling.

"So, for the last five years prior to our visit, he had made the question of the day a part of his morning meditation."

Carrie continued, "The fun-loving professor turned to me, who was a Psychology major, and said, 'Can you imagine a Theology professor actually walking–the–talk and praying each day?'

"At this we all laughed again!"

Carrie added, "I loved the one class I took with him. He had a way of helping me see and feel how much God really loves me."

Then Bill picked up the story, "Then the Professor took out a piece of paper. He told us, when he knew we were coming, he wrote down four of his *favorite 'Aha's'* from his meditations that related to the True Love That Lasts questions."

The First "Aha!"

Jesus's First Miracle

"The professor turned to me and said, 'Bill, the first Aha is Jesus's first miracle. Do you remember what it was?'

"I was delighted I remembered it was turning water into wine at the marriage at Cana.

"He pointed out that the situation Jesus picked for his first miracle was more than an accident. It highlights both *the importance of marriage* and how Jesus wanted the young couple to have a *very happy marriage day* by not letting the wine run out.

The Second "Aha!"

Propagation of the Human Race

"*His second Aha* was the fact that the Love of Union, when carried out sexually in marriage is the critical key to *the continuance of the human race itself.*

"He paused; then said, 'Think about that! Of all the options God had in creating us in His image and likeness, the Love of Union is the one He chose to continue the human race.'"

The Third "Aha!"
God Dwells In Those Who Keep His Word

Now Carrie jumped in. "Bill and I agreed that I get to tell you of the Third Aha because it meant so much to me.

"To understand the full importance to me, we need to go back to how the Professor said God solved the problem of free will and returning His love. He wants us to love Him in return for his love, but to be True Love, it has to be freely given. So, being the infinite gambler, God gave us free will. We could say 'No!' to God's love. But his ace in the hole was to love us so much and give us so many benefits that it would be irrational to say 'No!' to God's love.

"The Professor said, 'Because God wants us to freely love Him, he asks: 'Exactly as you are this moment, will you let me love you—NOW?'

"The Professor in our private meeting pointed out that it was like God was saying, 'Exactly as you are this moment, I want to love you.' But He is not going to let us continue in the imperfect state we were in that moment. He is committed to our continued improvement.

"*His Third Aha* was his favorite Gospel quote, John 14:23 when Jesus said, *If a man loves me, he will keep my word; and my Father will love him, and we will come to him and make our home with him.*

"The Professor pointed out our desire to love each other a little more each day and improve our relationship was *keeping His—God's—word.*

"The Professor asked us, besides the love of God, what is the next most important part of keeping God's word? Certainly the love of neighbor.

"And what 'neighbor' is more important to start with than your own spouse?

"He turned to me. I remember his exact words to this day. He said, 'Carrie, you and Bill have every right to be convinced the God dwelling within you wants to guide and help you answer and live the True Love That Lasts question each day. As my presentation emphasized, He has a vested interest in your success, especially your marital success.'"

There was a thoughtful pause respecting this life–changing insight Carrie wanted to share."

The Last "Aha!"
God Is Rejoicing In You

Very respectfully Bill continued, "The Professor pointed out his *Last Aha* is poetic, romantic and assures you that God's help and guidance will be there if you ask. It was a quote from Isaiah (62:4–5)

And as a bridegroom rejoices in his bride,
so shall your God rejoice in you.

"The Professor then slowly repeated his four Aha's, so we could consider how the flow showed God's intent. He then gave Carrie the sheet that he had prepared when he knew we were meeting."

Forever and Ever
...And Then Some

1. ***Jesus's first miracle***
   The happiness of a married couple at Cana

2. ***The Key to Continue the Human Race***
   The sexual expression of the Love of Union

3. ***God Dwells in Those Who Keep His Word,***
   i.e. He will personally help you keep His word, especially growing the love of your spouse daily.

4. ***God is Rejoicing in You***
   as a bridegroom rejoices over his bride.

Bill continued, "After a pause to review the four Aha's, the Professor said it was clear to him that the vague sensation Carrie and I were feeling as we prepared to cel-ebrate our tenth anniversary was a mistake many make.

"Most see the finding a partner, marring a partner and living with a partner as a fantastic happy journey. But many forget that every journey has a beginning and an end.

"I said to the Professor that he was certainly correct from my experience of finding Carrie, getting her to say 'yes' by the end of our Semester at Sea, getting married and living together. These ten years have certainly been a fantastic, happy journey.

"But I did not see the vague feelings we were missing as related to the beginning and end of our journey.

"I paused. The professor didn't say a word. He just looked at me intently as if he was waiting for me to ask a question. Then I asked him, what is this *beginning and end of the journey* you say we and many are forgetting?"

"With a brilliant compliment he pointed out our huge mistake. He said our dissertation and the True Love That Lasts questions are great insights, even brilliant insights. The questions have helped and will help many.

"But the very questions themselves just focus on the middle of our journey. The questions overlook the beginning and end of our journey.

"He said our journey began before time when God thought of us. Then according to science about 13.5 billion years ago the love of God went into action. He created and began preparing a home for Carrie and me. God also prepared for the end of our journey, which is our being happy with Him for eternity.

"He paused again to let that sink in."

"The Professor concluded, building on his personal experience, these four Aha's, and what we shared with him, what we are missing is obvious and very simple.

"I remember his exact words to this day. He said:

'1. In my presentation I showed God's vested interest in your success.

2. This means especially your marital success.

3. If you choose to ask the True Love That Lasts question of the day, God wants to partner the answers with you. Your mistake is not letting Him be your *Divine Partner.*'"

Carrie jumped in. "I remember that exact moment, and the look on Bill's face. He was speechless. And that does not happen too often."

At that, they all laughed.

Maria asked, "Bill, so what did you do?"

Bill replied, "I was speechless because I realized he was so right. We were trying to answer the daily question all alone. So I simply asked the Professor how he lets God be his Divine Partner when he asks the question of the day.

"True to the professor's brilliance, he had a very simple, easy to use answer. He said, he just adds, *Loving Partner God* to the beginning of each question."

There was another long pause.

Bill continued "As I see it today—for some 45 plus years now—his very simple suggestion of adding *Loving Partner God* to each question joins *three powers:*

1. It retains the power of asking the right question at the right time.

2. It has the power Maria wants: quick to learn, easy to use, proven to work.

3. It adds the power of the vested interest of our Divine Partner.

"Looking back, I was most impressed with the fact that Carrie and I went to our tenth anniversary reunion *with a vague problem.* We returned with *a Divine Partner.*

"Also, I know my own weaknesses. One of them is starting things with great excitement and clear intentions. And then not following through! So when we returned from the Tenth Reunion, I made myself a reminder sheet that I could use at the beginning of each day.

"This reminder sheet has been so helpful to me to start my day remembering to ask the question of the day and the fact that we have a Divine Partner, that I made you both a copy. Here it is:

What is True Love?

Can it grow?

Can it grow in a simple way?

Can it grow daily?

Beginning My Day With my Divine Partner

Monday/Wednesday

Loving Partner God, how can I appreciate and value the one I love more today?

Tuesday/Friday

Loving Partner God, how can I please and surprise the one I love more today?

Wednesday/Saturday

Loving Partner God, how can I be closer to and united with the one I love more today?

To our Tenth Reunion:

We went with a *vague problem*

We returned with a ***Divine Partner***

Accepting the copy, John said, "So this is the *so very simple* key that helped you impress your children and friends so much that they insisted on telling the world on your 55th Anniversary Cake.

"That article in the paper was so impressive to Maria and me that I keep a copy in my wallet."

He pulled out his wallet and showed them the article that brought them together.

Still The Young Couple After 55 Years

The friends and children of Carrie and Bill Kimmel insisted this couple—even though married 55 years—deserves the title:

"Still The Young Couple"

because they seem more in love than newlyweds. Carrie and Bill say it is all due to *The Secret of Growing True Love That Lasts.* They feel it's given them a Crystal Marriage.

They say the Secret is built on their definition of True Love.

And they say the Secret is so quick to learn and easy to use, people would not believe them if they shared it; even though it has surely created outstanding success for them for 55+ years.

Because they fear people will misunderstand the simplicity of *The Secret of Growing True Love That Lasts,* they refuse to say more.

They did say if a couple has the right attitude and is willing to try the Secret for 30 days, they would act as their coaches.

Chapter 17

The Wedding and the 10:13 Surprise

As they were waiting for John to complete his notes, Carrie said to Maria, "We would like to get back together in about six months to celebrate your progress. I would like to end your visit today with two questions:

"First, when is the wedding? Secondly, can we count on an invitation?"

Maria immediately answered, "To the second question, absolutely.

"To the first, to be decided."

A Month Later

As usual, Carrie opened the mail. She handed it to Bill and pointed out the part that read:

> *Come share with us the beginning*
> *of our commitment to build*
> *True Love That Lasts and*
> *Enjoy a Crystal Marriage*

She said, "That is a wonderful way to put it because we know what it means.

"I wonder what it means to others. I wonder if John will explain what it means at the wedding or reception."

After a pause to think, Bill reviewed their coaching experience, "John and Maria were special, as all our couples are. But they seem to excel in clarifying what they really want and taking immediate action to get it. Like crystal, they are very transparent to each other and us."

Carrie added, "Also like crystal, they take the light from each other and make it sparkle, helping each other grow. When you flick crystal, it makes a special, clear sound. Listening to them, they have a commitment to make their marriage special, like crystal is special."

Bill added the scientific. "Crystal glass differs from regular glass at the molecular level. In regular glass the molecules are random. The strength and purity of sound of the crystal comes from the very orderly line-up of the molecules.

"John's very essence was orderly as he took notes. Maria was very orderly in the questions she asked.

"I'm looking forward to going to their wedding and experiencing more of how they live their desire for a Crystal Marriage."

Carrie replied, "I'm with you!" as she put the date on their calendar in red.

Three Months Later

Before Bill and Carrie knew it, the day came, and they were at the wedding.

Every aspect reflected John and Maria's dream—the music, the decorations, the flowers, the attendance...

But the part that Carrie and Bill found most meaningful and satisfying were the vows themselves.

It was obvious John and Maria both had given at lot of thought and prayer to their vows.

Each ended their commitment to the other with...

"...and with the help
of our ***Loving Partner, God,***
I will do all in my power asking
the True Love That Lasts
question of the day
to make ours a ***Crystal Marriage.****"*

The reception was also over the top, with heavy emphasis on omnipresent crystal.

They selected a banquet hall that had a gigantic crystal chandelier with smaller crystal chandeliers in many places.

The glasses for the toast were crystal. Their clear sound rang many times when the friends tapped them demanding a kiss by the bride and groom.

The cake said,

"To the Crystal Marriage of our Dream."

John gave a very well-prepared presentation of their experience from the Starbucks' 'not now John!' to the final 'yes.'

He made a special point to share what Maria learned from Dan Beuthner at the convention: *If you have a reason to get up tomorrow, you can add years to your longevity.*

John then said, "There are two very important things I would like all to know." He paused to indicate something very important was coming.

"A very important thing I have to get up for each of my tomorrows is: to ask and answer the True Love That Lasts question of the day so tomorrow is a continuous improvement step creating this Crystal Marriage with this diamond of a wife for the next 55+ years."

He was immediately interrupted by all the crystal glasses tinkling the demand for the couple to kiss. Glad to respond, they did just that.

He then continued, "*The other thing* I want to point out is a living example of research that says if you have a good reason to get up tomorrow you can add years to your longevity.

"I'd like you to give our coaches a standing ovation. They taught us the True Love That Lasts questions. And because they use them daily, their children and friends insisted that their 55th anniversary cake say ***Still The Young Couple."***

The attendees were very glad to oblige.

Bill and Carrie were very pleased to be invited to the breakfast for the families and bridal party the next morning.

At breakfast, Maria's little six-year old niece and nephew twins were directed to deliver Bill and Carrie a note.

> Bill and Carrie,
>
> Our limousine takes us to the airport shortly after 10:15 a.m. from the front of the hotel.
>
> Could you meet us there at 10:00 a.m. to say goodbye? We have something special to show you.
>
> Thanking you in advance,
> John

Promptly at 10:00 a.m., Bill and Carrie arrived at the front of the hotel to say their goodbyes and wish the newlyweds well.

At exactly 10:13 a.m. both John and Maria's cell phones went off. Both pulled their cells from their personal bags and let Bill and Carrie enjoy the Crystal ring of the reminder call.

John began the planned explanation. "Both our cell phones are set for 10:13 a.m. and p.m., 10:13 because it was at exactly that time, I first saw this drop-dead gorgeous girl, who is now my wife."

Maria continued the planned thank you, "10:13 a.m. to check that we have already asked the True Love That Lasts question of the day. At 10:13 p.m. to remind us to make a note of the discovery or action taken.

Then together they said with a huge smile of success,

"We're not going to break the chain."

Forever and Ever
...And Then Some

The Beginning Of Maria and John's Growing True Love That Lasts Into A Crystal Marriage

Appendix

Forever and Ever
...And Then Some

Critical Basics in Review

The Symbol

The book's symbol, like the book and life itself, can be viewed from two vantage points—***The Present*** and ***The Big Picture.***

The Present

Viewing the symbol from the present vantage point, the **heart** stands for one of our most basic desires: to love and be loved.

"True Love" reminds us that when we love and are loved, we want it to be love that is ***true***.

Once we experience True Love and ponder it deeper, we want this True Love to be infinite, symbolized by the infinity sign "**∞**", i.e. a figure with no ending. Desiring infinite True Love can generate a double meaning in the human heart. The first meaning is unconditional love, a True Love that is possible even in this life. The second desire is for your love to be never ending. To be *really never ending,* we need to go to the good news of the Big Picture.

The Big Picture

"Forever and Ever...And Then Some" reminds us of the very good news of *The Big Picture.* Looking at life from the vantage point of *The Big Picture* reminds us that we are created in the image and likeness of our God, Who is—as St. John says—Love Himself. After a time enjoying the love of those we are close to here in this limited life, we will go back to our God of Love, from whence we came. There we will enjoy the love of those we love now, and most especially *our God Who is infinite Love* ***"Forever and Ever ... And Then Some."***

An "Aha" Bonus From Our Advisory Team

This symbol, like every other part of the book, was reviewed by our advisory team. The first member of the team said the infinity symbol "**∞**" looks like you are looking at love through glasses. Then this "Aha" bonus jumped out. The symbol can also remind you that when you look at *True Love* through *infinite glasses,* you are seeing as God—who is infinite Love—sees, a God who has a vested interest in your marital success. (cf. Ch. 15 & 16)

Three Suggestions for a Quick Start And Immediate Benefits

If you would like a quick start to a lifelong path to value and enjoy the relationship with your spouse more daily—or any person important to you—here are three suggestions.

1. The True Love That Lasts Questions

Monday/Thursday Ch. 9
How can I appreciate and value the one I love more today?

Tuesday/Friday Ch. 10
How can I please and surprise the one I love more today?

Wednesday/Saturday Ch. 11
How can I be closer to and united with the one I love more today? Remember, these questions are built on *true love,* Ch. 6

2. A Common Danger and Tips to Overcome It

Many people begin to use the True Love That Lasts questions, but don't built the habit and lose the lifetime benefits.

Tips

a. *Keep score* on a calendar placed where you have your first cup of coffee and meditate. See Ch. 12 & 13

b. Keep a short record of the discovery/action taken each day. This will help you be more accountable to yourself. It will help grow the value of the one you love. It will give you a record to see your progress.

c. Set a morning alarm to remind you to ask the question and an evening alarm to keep the record.

3. Invite your Spouse (the One You Love) to join you

As Chapter 10 shows, there are significant benefits when you use the daily questions alone. However, if your spouse will join you, you create synergism: 1 + 1 > 3.

This synergistic effect helps bonding and grows your relationship.

Quick Start to Take Your Crystal Marriage To a More Realistic, Even Divine Level

More Realistic Ch. 15

Fact 1. There was a time when you were not.

Fact 2. Today you are because of a gratuitous gift from God and the cooperation of your parents. For this reason, both God and your parents have a *vested interest in you* and *your successful marriage.*

Conclusion: Your view is more realistic when you acknowledge your Creator as your Partner with a vested interest in *your successful marriage.*

Divine Level Ch. 16

Conclusion: Since your Creator has a vested interest in your successful marriage and wants to be your Partner, invite Him to partner your answer each day to the True Love That Lasts question.

Monday/Wednesday Ch. 8–9

Loving Partner God, how can I appreciate and value the one I love more today?

Tuesday/Friday Ch. 10

Loving Partner God, how can I please and surprise the one I love more today?

Wednesday/Saturday Ch. 11

Loving Partner God, how can I be closer to and united with the one I love more today?

Benefits You Can Expect

God told us to love our neighbor as ourselves. A very important place to start is with your spouse or the one you love.

Asking for His help as a Partner, you don't lose any of the simplicity of the daily True Love That Lasts questions.

You add Divine power and guidance to the answer.

Getting The Most From The Secret of Growing True Love That Lasts

Fact

You will get more for yourself when you share these *True Love That Lasts* ideas and insights with those you care about.

Question

Who in the following list would most appreciate and benefit from your sharing or giving them this book? The book makes a great gift, whether it's for a special occasion such as a birthday or for Christmas/Hanukkah, or for someone you think will enjoy the benefits this book offers.

Spouse ______________________________

Girlfriend ______________________________

Boyfriend ______________________________

Mother ______________________________

Father ______________________________

Son(s) ______________________________

Daughter(s) ______________________________

Brother(s) ______________________________

Sisters (s) ______________________________

Cousins(s) ______________________________

In Laws (s) ______________________________

Other Relative(s) ______________________________

Friend ______________________________

Coworker ______________________________

Boss/Manager ______________________________

Student ______________________________

Teacher ______________________________

Doctor ______________________________

Other ______________________________

____

____

____

____

Special Appreciations

Ken Blanchard It is difficult to adequately acknowledge Ken's influence in my life and the life of my co–author, Carol. He encouraged and inspired every aspect of this book.

Rob Neate and Cathy Koch of Puget Sound Energy Rob and Cathy discussed for over a year each chapter with great insight and encouragement.

Irene Kaufman who tirelessly corrected and encouraged the many drafts of True Love That Lasts.

Thanks to *Bishop Caggiano* of the Bridgeport Diocese for his recognizing that the True Love That Lasts single question a day is a very simple recipe for a strong, healthy marriage. We also thank him for thinking enough of the book to take a copy to Pope Francis.

Thanks to *Patrick Donovan,* Executive Director of the Leadership Institute for recognizing the book and the single question a day as a valuable support for Pre–Cana and other marriage preparation programs.

The *True Love That Lasts* Advisory Team

This Advisory Team comes from many walks of life: old friends, business clients, fellow authors and Deacon Jeff Font's Immaculate High School students, who participated in a four-week discussion group of every aspect of the book. Their feedback helped make this book all it is. I especially appreciate their input. I queried the Team over fifty times for their insights.

Barenblitt, Alex
Biermann, Alicia
Biker, Alan
Bono, Victoria
Bourasa, Kimberly
Braxton, Dr. Cheryl
Campo, Alissa
Carew, Fr. Larry
Carr, Roger
Conway, Ray
Crocker, Rev. George
Cutting, Bob
Desmarais, Dave
Despagna, Natalia
Doering, Andrew
Doherty, Ailene
Donio, Celia
Donovan, Patrick
Elmore, Dr. Elizabeth
Fanella, Caitlin
Flanagan, Kara
Font, Deacon Jeff
Garvey, Grace
Gibbons, Sue
Hahn, Eileen
Henson, Roger
Herceg, Dan
Hill, Bob
Jennings, Pat
Kent, Peter
Kirkman, Hunter
Kroll, Greg
Lauri, George
LeFebvre, Kristen
Liguzinski, Tom
Lock, Timothy G.
McCorquodale, Charlette
McGinn, Greg
McKenna Meryl
Miezin, Casey
Monti, Carl
Moradian, Nancy
Musharbash, Ray
Myers, Dillard
Parry, Bill
Piegat, Travis
Quartaro, Elisa
Richards, Ray
Roeder, Jeff
Scarabino, Mario
Serviss, Scott
Staelgraeve, Mark & MaryEllen
Suess, Jennifer & David
Sweeny, Liz
Taney, Mike
Timm, Bart
Torres, Cheri
Vitarbo, Lin
Wesner, Prof. John
Wichert, Tom
Williams, Debra
Winkley, Don

Other Resources To Get The Most from Your Time, Life, and Career

Ever Present Challenges	Wished For Benefits
Too much to do! I never get everything done!	Accomplish more, especially important tasks
Too many interruptions	Increase satisfaction
Not enough personal or family time	Greater work/life balance
Too little control over my life	The ability to live a fuller more fulfilling life
Too much stress	Optimize Happiness

If you can relate to one or all of the *Ever Present Challenges* or the *Wished For Benefits,* we suggest you check Jim's international Best Seller *Aligned Thinking: Make Every Moment Count.*

Coming Soon

Get the Most From Your Time, Life, and Career

by Jim Steffen

In paperback and audiobook.

Other Resources
To Grow Your True Love That Lasts

The Secret of Growing True Love That Lasts is now available in:

Paperback
Audiobook
Kindle

Visit: **www.TrueLoveThatLasts.us** for more help, tips and hints and to receive your FREE Discussion Guide for the book.

Coming Soon

Teleseminar ***Growing True Love That Lasts***—details on the web site **www.TrueLoveThatLasts.us.**

Speakers Available

The co–authors are available for presentations, retreats, days of recollection, and business events.

For more resources, see the following page and visit **www.TrueLoveThatLasts.us.**

About the Co-authors Jim & Carol Steffen

R. James (Jim) Steffen spent the early part of his life earning four degrees: Philosophy, Theology, Mathematics and Educational Psychology. This helped him found SSA International (Steffen, Steffen & Associates, Inc.). As President of SSA International, Dr. Jim became an internationally known speaker, consultant, and trainer. This gave him opportunity to work with leaders in 160 Fortune 500 Companies over the last 40+ years.

His company and management programs helped many clients get the most from their time and career. He summarized these discoveries and insights in his international best seller: *Aligned Thinking: Make Every Moment Count.* It was translated into seven languages. But something was still missing: how to get the most from life and love itself.

It was only when he met and married his co-author, Carol Steffen that he learned from her how *"life can be better than a dream come true."* She also helped him realize that True Love That Lasts can be *Forever and Ever and Then Some,* indicating that it can last even into the next life.

As married partners for thirty–three plus years, they have teamed up to share with you how the simplicity of a *single question a day* can help you discover and implement...*The Secret of Growing True Love That Lasts.*

For more information visit: www.TrueLoveThatLasts.us

CPSIA information can be obtained
at www.ICGtesting.com
Printed in the USA
FSHW021837210220

9 781087 867342